8: Europe in the Age of Negotiation

THE WASHINGTON PAPERS
Volume I

8: Europe in the
Age of Negotiation

Pierre Hassner

THE CENTER FOR STRATEGIC AND INTERNATIONAL STUDIES
Georgetown University, Washington, D.C.

 SAGE PUBLICATIONS
Beverly Hills / London

For information address:

SAGE PUBLICATIONS, INC.
275 South Beverly Drive
Beverly Hills, California 90212

SAGE PUBLICATIONS LTD
St George's House / 44 Hatton Garden
London EC1N 8ER

International Standard Book Number 0-8039-0281-6

Library of Congress Catalog Card No. 73-83410

FIRST PRINTING

*When citing a Washington Paper, please use the proper form. Remember to cite
the series title and include the paper number. One of the two following formats
can be adapted (depending on the style manual used):*

(1) HASSNER, P. (1973) "Europe in the Age of Negotiation." The Washington
Papers, I, 8. Beverly Hills and London: Sage Pubns.

OR

(2) Hassner, Pierre. 1973. *Europe in the Age of Negotiation.* The Washington
Papers, vol. 1, no. 8. Beverly Hills and London: Sage Publications.

CONTENTS

INTRODUCTION

INTRODUCTION

The first part of this paper deals primarily with Western Europe's relationship to the United States; the second part deals with Western Europe's relationship to Eastern Europe. While the first is more concerned with security and the second with political change, they are both focused toward one complex phenomenon: the transformation of power in today's international world and its consequences for the possibilities of a West European foreign policy.

This transformation can be seen as a change in the structure of power—hence the discussions, in the first part, of the passing of bipolarity and the doubtful emergence of a five-power balance. It can also be seen as a change in the nature of power—hence the discussion, in the second part, of the increasingly important indirect influence of domestic societies upon each other. In both cases, the role of, and the consequences for, Western Europe are absolutely central. Like Japan, only even more so, Europe is a potential great power that may always remain potential. Like Japan, only more so, Europe may have a chance—perhaps born of necessity—of becoming what Francois Duchêne has called the world's first civilian center of power.

But doesn't "civilian" mean primarily "economic?" In trying to answer this question, the weakness of this paper and its message are both revealed.

AUTHOR'S NOTE: *This paper draws heavily on two earlier works: (1) a paper I presented at the Conference on European Security, SALT, and U.S.-European Relations, sponsored by the Carnegie Endowment for International Peace and held in Geneva from August 31 to September 2, 1972, under the title, "Between Two Ages or Between Two Stools? The Implications of Political Change for European Security and Arms Control;" and (2) an article I published in the French monthly,* Esprit, *December 1972, under the title, "L'Europe de l'Est, Vue de Loin."*

It is obvious that to speak of Europe's situation and role without giving more than implicit or passing attention to the economic dimension is a huge limitation, one which characterizes this paper primarily because of the author's lack of competence. Obviously, the only respect in which Western Europe does constitute a power is the economic one: it is mainly through this sphere that she irritates her Western allies and attracts her Eastern neighbors. The transatlantic bargain, as seen by the United States and by many West Europeans, is one of military protection against economic concessions; the East-West dialogue, as seen by the communist countries, consists in accepting certain risks of cultural and ideological penetration against hopes of technological and economic assistance. In both cases, Western Europe's leverage is primarily economic; her vulnerability is primarily tied to the political insecurity of being militarily dependent upon the protection of an increasingly distant ally or the good will of an increasingly present continental neighbor. In both cases, what counts is the relation between economic and military power, and its interplay with the crucial third dimension: social health and political will.

The necessity for this writer to concentrate on the latter political sphere may have the virtue of counterbalancing the trends by which quite sensible critics of past illusions now seem in danger of being carried away themselves. On the one hand, it is healthy to learn from the tragedy of misapplied military power in Vietnam and from the nuclear stalemate. But to argue (as does, for example, Robert Hunter) that economic power has simply replaced military power, is merely to fall back into an American illusion familiar since the days of the Founding Fathers, and to ignore the ever more subtle and complex interplay of military, economic, and political power. On the other hand, while the older belief in Western European economic power being automatically translated into economic and political unity probably was a form of wishful thinking, Americans, once they have discovered that this development would not necessarily be beneficial to their interests, may either exaggerate its dangers or fall into a new form of wishful thinking. Americans may come to believe—as some of the excellent contributors to the January

1973 issue of *Foreign Affairs* seem to do—that Europe can never find the inner strength for reacting to external challenges, and this just at a time when a certain convergence of policies in the face of the various superpower challenges is beginning to be felt.

Of course this means neither that Western Europe can or should become a fourth or fifth superpower, nor that, everything being possible, we must rest content with the infinite complexity, ambiguity, and unpredictability of human and particularly international affairs. On the contrary, what it does mean is that in Western Europe's relations both with Eastern Europe, and even more, perhaps, with the United States, deep changes are inevitable, but the nature and direction of these changes is not. Even if the causes of change are economic or military, its meaning remains to be defined by the political choice of the Europeans themselves as well as by that of the outside powers.

In this respect, the seventies are likely to be even more decisive than "coming years" are normally proclaimed to be. By 1980, either Western Europe will be capable of autonomous, even if limited, action in commercial, monetary, political and, to some extent, military matters; or the degree of integration already achieved (for instance, in areas like agricultural policy) will break down under the pressure of divergent interests, or will be diluted in a generalized interdependence, or both.

The European summit of October 1972 and various bilateral dialogues involving France—traditionally the European country most reluctant to integrate—have freely proclaimed and reaffirmed European union as the first goal of these countries' policies, and economic and monetary union as the next step and the test of progress toward this union. Now perhaps this is not to be taken seriously, although one may wonder why these governments would go into precise commitments and timetables in the absence of internal and external constraints if they did not mean to keep them. But if they do, this will obviously involve a greater degree of political union than some of them seem prepared to accept today.

Whatever the way out of this contradiction, there can be only one conclusion. Seven or ten years from now, Western Europe will certainly not be a fifth superpower in the same class as the first three, nor even probably the first four. Even if it does progress on the road to unity, it will probably still be in a transitional phase, full of problems, conflicts, and crises; but if it does not progress enough to be able to adopt a common policy towards the outside world in certain key areas, its existing degree of unity will disintegrate and its member countries will fall into the economic orbit of the United States, or the military orbit of the Soviet Union, or both.

One can distinguish four or five directions based on existing trends and leading to four possible Europes.

(1) A Europe dominated by superpower collaboration would be encouraged not only by the strategic dialogue, but also by certain economic tendencies which sometimes seem to lead to a great Soviet-American bargain based on a certain complementarity of interests.

(2) A Europe dominated by the United States would result, in particular, from the dynamism of multinational—but primarily American—corporations. If American economic penetration is strengthened and, at the same time, extended to Eastern Europe, not so much through commerce as through industrial cooperation, if the dollar remains at the center of the international monetary system, if European economic unity is weaker than internal conflicts and external ties, if at the same time the Soviet Union and Eastern Europe are going through a period of crisis or economic difficulties or, simply, of paralysis, some aspects of this type of Europe may become real.

(3) A Europe dominated by the Soviet Union could happen if, as in the first two models, the Nine do not succeed in reaching common policies, and this failure takes place in the context of an economic conflict with the United States and of a partial military withdrawal of the latter, as well as of intra-West European bickering. If on the other hand, the Soviet Union is in a period of both increasing military strength and diplomatic activism, and succeeds in dominating the new pan-European institutions by leading a comparatively united socialist commonwealth while

other European states are disunited and the United States and Canada are pushed into a marginal role by the trend of the discussions, by the nature of the joint pan-European projects and, above all, by their own disengagement or disinterest, then this Europe would be dominated by the Soviet Union psychologically and diplomatically even if it is dominated economically by the Common Market.

(4) A European, or balanced Europe could come about if:

(a) Western, Eastern, neutral and nonaligned European states increase the relative importance of their mutual ties without breaking their ties with their respective superpowers or even less getting into conflict with them;

(b) Western Europe, without becoming as powerful as the United States economically or as the Soviet Union militarily, does acquire enough weight to prevent an exclusive domination from either direction;

(c) small and middle-sized East European countries succeed in showing a certain independence from Russia and a certain community of views among themselves within subregional and pan-European organizations;

(d) the United States and Soviet Union understand that, in their own interest as well as in that of the continent, it is preferable to have a moderate political influence on the whole region, albeit with specific and stronger ties to their respective half but without any special right of intervention, rather than a direct and exclusive economic, military, or ideological domination.

If all this happens, then the perennial dilemma of the European balance (Western Europe without the United States is too strong facing Eastern Europe without the Soviet Union, but too weak facing Eastern Europe plus the Soviet Union) may begin to be resolved through the peaceful coexistence, and varying degrees of cooperation and alliance, between various powers and organizations.

And yet, from the United States and the Soviet Union to most of the underdeveloped countries, everybody (except China and the associates of the EEC) seems to fear that the Common Market and European union might lead to the creation of a closed bloc or a new superpower that would be aggressive or expansionist, both economically and militarily. In fact, they are fighting a straw man that corresponds neither to the aspirations nor to the means of the Nine, who all know that they have no interest either in a dollar crisis, or in an international trade crisis, or in a return to the Cold War.

For whatever it is worth, Western Europe is inevitably carried along by the double network of relationships constituted by the capitalist-based world economic system and by the détente-based East-West European system. Europe cannot resist, whether economically or politically, the dynamics of interpenetration, especially if they are practiced by her partners. This is all the more so since her internal situation—domestic priorities, social crises, the lack of a state-like unity—preclude her becoming a nuclear superpower or practicing a conventional military (e.g., naval) policy of armed intervention or gunboat diplomacy.

But only European unity has a chance of avoiding a much likelier danger: that of a fragmented Europe which externally would correspond to one or several of the first three models and whose states would essentially turn their attention inward to their respective domestic crises, i.e., to the sterile and monotonous confrontation of authoritarians without authority, of revolutionaries without revolution, and of reformers without reforms. Outside again, these same states would be driven in separate directions by their rivalries, inequalities, and resentments, as well as by the desire for safeguarding their security or their commercial ties—some more into the political sphere of the Soviet Union, others into the economic one of the United States.

As only a united Europe would be able to acquire a real independence, it alone would be able to search for an original model of political purpose and organization. In relation to the outside world, it would mostly try to safeguard its own freedom of social experimentation and to help others to achieve it. Its priorities would necessarily be civilian and social. From a political-military point of view, it would be essentially defensive: it would seek above all enough weight not to be subjected —whether within the Atlantic alliance or within the new pan-European system—to the hegemony of the mightiest. Like the German Confederation in the nineteenth century, it would have to be strong enough to keep its independence, but could not be united enough to be able to follow an offensive policy. From a political-economic point of view, it could certainly not aspire to building a new empire, of dual domination in Eastern Europe, not even in the Mediterranean countries: the influence of the Soviet Union, of the United States, or of both, would be sure to prevent it. Our time is not favorable to closed spheres of influence; where they might subsist, it is not Western Europe who could deny access to external powers. Quite the contrary, its regional role, to the east or to the south, could be precisely to encourage the independence of smaller countries by helping them to avoid a unilateral dependence and to accede to the main form of economic independence in the age of interpenetration—namely, the diversification and the balancing of interdependencies.

There is no fruitful cooperation without some form of reciprocity, and there is no real reciprocity without some form of equality. But if Europe is to make a positive contribution by giving a more balanced structure to international cooperation, it must first be allowed to exist. The nature and orientation of European unity is a matter of international debate. Just as the changes of the international environment have a powerful stimulating, deterrent, or distracting effect on European unification, so the latter must at every step take into account its effects, good or bad, on everyone else. But this is different from granting outsiders any kind of veto right. External acquiescence is essential, but cannot be bought at the price of internal identity. On the contrary, the latter is the precondition for successful cooperation and interpenetration.

It has been obvious for sometime that international economic relations had to be seen as the management and the manipulation of a common system, and that, in order to function without falling into crises and producing conflicts, this system had to become more balanced. The meaning of SALT may be that strategic relations will increasingly be seen in this light: as the management of a common system of security, rather than of a hostile confrontation. The problem will then be to avoid tensions and misunderstandings between a powerful and closed elite of security producers and a mass of powerless and distrustful security consumers. Finally, the meaning of the Conference on Security and Cooperation in Europe as a process may also be that social, cultural, and economic interaction and interpenetration in Europe have to be both encouraged, protected, and controlled if crises and regressions are to be avoided.

Monetary events remind us all too often that "management" does not exclude manipulation. A common interest in the maintenance of these three systems or processes of strategic, economic, and social interdependence does not mean that each of them (and even more, the relations among the three) do not involve a constant competition for influence and control. But this jockeying for strategic positions in the management of a common system or of a long-range process has more to do with the combination of diversity and cooperation associated with a concert than with either the rigidities of a bipolar balance or the acrobatics of a flexible one.

It is the contention of this European writer that in all these three areas the interests not only of Europe but of the system as a whole would best be served by a more multilateral or balanced management than would be afforded by unilateral American decisions (as seems sometimes the case in monetary matters), or by a bipolar Soviet-American control (as may be feared in strategic ones), or by an anarchic mixture of unchecked Soviet pressures and of unrestrained U.S. reactions.

At any rate, the task of going beyond false dilemmas (e.g., isolationism versus imperialism, an obsolete and oppressive bipolarity versus a premature and dangerous five-power balance, submission versus confrontation, drift versus adventure) is a challenge to both the courage and the moderation, of a Europe and an America in a world where becoming more different and more independent makes it more imperative than ever to understand and adjust to each other's evolution.

PART I.

Facing West:
An Emancipated America?

"Plus C'est la Même Chose, Plus ca Change"

Europe is the most stable of continents. Among the
dimensions of the European situation, the military one is
the most stable of all. And yet the "winds of change" and the
"era of negotiation" have obviously reached the continent, and
the security dimension constitutes, directly or indirectly, either
the theme or a crucial element of these negotiations.

A double paradox is involved here. Clearly, Europeans have
never been less afraid of war, yet this is the time for negotiations
about European security. They are made possible and necessary
not by a situation of insecurity, but by one of détente. In turn,
this détente is based on the status quo. Yet it is inseparable from
expectations of change. The negotiations themselves reflect basic
changes in the relations among the three major European
powers—the Soviet Union, the United States, and Germany—as
well as uncertainties as to whether the enlarged European
community represents an emerging new power. This uncertainty
by itself is already producing a change in the attitudes and
policies of the superpowers towards Europe.

In Europe, then, the "era of negotiation" may be healing old
wounds but creating new tensions. It may be an era of increased
opportunities and expectations but also, by the same token, of
increased unpredictability and instability. Europe has led the way
in the hostile bipolar stability imposed by the Cold War, but also

in the constructive stability resulting from reconciliation and attempts at community-building in the West. For a while, it seemed that the rest of the world might become Europeanized in this double sense. Today, it is Europe that seems to be becoming less different from other regions, less bipolar, but also less stable, more prone to interstate competition and to domestic social and political crises. The question is what difference do these changes in the general state and atmosphere of European politics make to the substance of European security?

It is difficult to disagree with the logic of the position—most powerfully expressed in two articles by Frederick Wyle (1972, 1970)—according to which there is neither any serious danger to the present conventional and strategic balance (whether through SALT or through Soviet superiority) nor any serious prospect of changing it (whether through negotiations with the East or through the total or partial substitution of a European deterrent for the American one or of nuclear weapons for conventional forces).

The problem arises when one goes from the short to the long run, and from technical realities to political perceptions and dynamics. If one defines "stability" less in terms of military security than in terms of popular consensus and confidence, or in terms of diplomatic alignments and their reliability, if one sees military postures and arms control arrangements primarily in terms of their influence on the maintenance, management, or manipulation of these political structures and processes—then it is precisely in a stable nuclear environment that strategy has to become most concerned with domestic pressures, economic constraints, and transnational trends.

European security and arms control objectives have to be seen in the light of the dialectical relationship between these three dimensions: the balance of military power, the interaction of foreign policies, and the evolution of societies.

Recent or likely shifts in the military balance are, at least in Europe, certainly meaningless for winning a war and almost certainly for avoiding it, but they can have an indirect impact on the other dimensions. Conversely, diplomatic initiatives and social turmoil have had little impact, so far, on the structure of the

European system, which is ultimately based on the mutual balance and the joint superiority of the two superpowers. But the changing characters of their relations with each other, with their allies or satellites, and with their own societies, are certainly altering the salience or the visible importance of the military balance; they may, in the long run, alter not only its political function and significance but its very structure.

In 1967, the writer thought that for the coming years, European security would be more a theme for political discussions and maneuvers than the object of a genuine search for alternative arrangements:

> Just as the tenuous détente and cooperation form part of a language on which each party tries to foster his own political objectives and to show that they are the best contribution to that particular value, so the debate on European security may turn not so much on the best way of achieving security as on *who* should achieve it against *whom* and in what framework. European security may constitute one of the languages and one of the forums for discussing the political future of Europe, of the German nation, or of East-West relations. If this is so, even such concrete issues as the Soviet MRBM or a European BMD system will probably take on this symbolic meaning in the continuing strategic debate between Western Europe, the United States and Russia.... [In the case of the European security system as of the nonproliferation treaty,] there may be in the making a permanent, very slightly veiled political discussion on the reordering of both the international system and the European one.
>
> The security dialogue will start by having the meaning of a signal in a double sense: it will indicate both the level reached by the economic, social, ideological and political transformation of Europe, and the limits beyond which this transformation cannot go without endangering the whole structure. If and when this last point is reached, the discussion about a European security system, which today is about the political future of Germany, of Europe, and of their relations with the United States and the Soviet Union, may yet turn to a new and surprisingly fresh subject: the problem of security [Hassner, 1968].

Are we approaching this point? Or is the function of the security dialogue still symbolic and subordinate? The answer cannot help being ambiguous, like the situation itself.

As preoccupations, there is no question that the security dimension of European relationships (both East-West and West-West) and the European dimension of strategic relations between superpowers are returning to the center of the stage after a relatively long eclipse.

After the end of the Berlin crisis and the exhaustion of the NATO debates (subsequent to the death of the MLF and the storm over the Non-Proliferation Treaty), a separation occurred between East-West relations in Europe and the problems of security and arms control.

There was a separation between European détente, conducted mainly by West European powers (France, then Germany) with the East (Eastern Europe and, increasingly, the Soviet Union) in nonmilitary terms, and superpower relations, first partly frozen by Vietnam, then focusing mainly on the global strategic relationship rather than any regional one, with the exception of the Middle East. Precisely because it seemed to concern essentially the superpowers themselves, SALT provoked much lower European anxieties than NPT. As for the United States-West European relationships it was frozen by Gaullist obstruction, American studied indifference and preoccupation with Vietnam, and Germany's new interest in the East. Now all these separate directions seem to come to life again and to converge.

The development of several bilateral relationships, leading to bilateral agreements and to a multilateral one on Berlin, has given birth to a new multilateral phase that raises the problem of their common framework. Ostpolitik and SALT were two relatively separate undertakings. But their respective achievements lead to their mutual Europeanization. Among the Conference on Security and Cooperation in Europe (CSCE), the Mutually Balanced Force Reductions (MBFR), and SALT II, immediate connections or overlaps, possible confusions or conflicts and necessary coordination are much more obvious. On the other hand, new trends in the United States and in Western Europe reopen the problem of a new balance in Western defense and, perhaps, of a new transatlantic relationship.

All these perspectives and debates, however, retain more than ever their character of shadow-boxing. The most striking aspect of the "era of negotiation" is that it consists mainly in recognizing the status quo. In Europe, the "era of negotiation" has begun in earnest only since 1969, when, in contrast to earlier periods where polycentric attempts failed against the rigidity of the system, all the main actors (the Soviet Union, West Germany, the United States, and however reluctantly, East Germany) have started to talk to each other. But the theme of the talks is much more "the recognition of existing realities" or "of the results of World War II" than "the dissolution of the blocs" or the creation of a European security system.

The Soviet Union feels confident to embark on a "Westpolitik" including Germany precisely because, through her intervention in Czechoslovakia, she has gained recognition for the firmness of her resolve to keep Eastern Europe, if necessary by force. She can gain ground in her dialogue with the West because she no longer presents a direct challenge to Berlin's link with the Federal Republic of Germany (FRG), the FRG's with the Common Market, and Europe's with the United States. Germany can embark on a dynamic Ostpolitik precisely because its substantive content consists of recognizing her division and, on the other hand, because she leaves no doubt on the maintenance of her West European and Atlantic ties and on the need to keep the American military presence in Europe. Even France has become an advocate of this presence and of the military status quo. For the United States itself, the Berlin agreement certainly was a reconfirmation of the status quo; whatever else SALT may be or become, the negotiations certainly are before everything, a recognition of parity and of mutual deterrence. This, certainly for the present administration, implies a need for scrupulous attention aimed at maintaining an overall strategic and European balance and at avoiding unilateral concessions or signs of weakness. Hence the solid resistance against pressures for unilateral troop withdrawals and a very cautious approach to MBFR.

Finally, as regards relations between the United States and Western Europe, while a shift of attitudes does exist (as witnessed by the remark attributed to Henry Kissinger: "The Kennedy administration had it all wrong: it encouraged European economic unity which could hurt American interests and discouraged

European military independence which could favor them"), it is likely that neither real economic conflict nor real military devolution will take place. Here too, then, the prospect is for the continuation of the present system, but with changes in atmosphere and in style, in emphasis and in balance.

The real question, now even more than in 1967, is whether these marginal or external changes are not in the long run likely to produce qualitative or structural changes in the system itself. If the main effect of negotiation is to recognize the status quo, the main effect of this recognition may well be to unleash forces that will undermine it more irresistably than either military pressure or diplomatic bargaining.

This does not mean that these forces of internal change or of interpenetration will necessarily win; various combinations are possible, from repression to regeneration, on one or on both sides. The point is that, contrary to a frozen bipolar confrontation or to a give-and-take negotiation, the competitive-cooperative management of a contradictory process of détente is essentially unpredictable, and that this long-range uncertainty —while not necessarily harmful to the deterrence of nuclear war—does create new problems for a security system based on alliances and alignments born in a different age and environment. In the East, it may create the dialectics of communication and *Abgrenzung,* of emancipation and repression. In the West, it may encourage the dialectics of "decoupling" and "Finlandization" or the reciprocal fear of unilateral accommodation.

The central characteristic of the European security system has been the continuity between, so to speak, Berlin and the strategic nuclear balance: the correspondence between, on the one hand, the geographical division and the ideological opposition of the two Germanies, the two Europes, the two social systems; and, on the other hand, the military balance between the two superpowers materialized by their alliance organizations, their physical presence, and their nuclear weapons. Any trend that puts into question the unity of the respective sides, their mutual opposition, or the relevance of the military balance to this opposition obviously creates problems of adaptation. Not only a bureaucratic organization like NATO, but the security system it is part of can, in the long run, be made to look anachronistic by détente with the East, by dissension within the West, and, more generally, by the transformation of the international system (whether in the direction of multipolarity or of superpower condominium) and of the relations between society and defense, or between domestic trends and foreign policy.

Détente may make defense establishments and opposing alliances look either obsolete or positively harmful to the process of reconciliation. To Europeans, the American connection or a defense effort to supplement or replace it, may appear as an obstacle to further progress toward reunification; to Americans, the objections of European allies may appear as an obstacle to further progress toward bilateral arms control agreements with the Soviet Union. Dissension within the West, even if it does not lead to separation and should rationally not supersede the real elements of convergence in security interests between the two sides of the Atlantic, still encourages an increasingly divergent perception of these interests. A security link seen by both sides as a necessary evil standing in the way of more positively appealing aspirations may continue through inertia or prudence, but cannot help being affected negatively in its credibility and its efficiency. NATO—including a certain American presence in Europe—may remain; but the level of U.S. troops, the character of NATO strategy, and the possibilities of constructive reform in the respective American and European roles would certainly vary. Technical issues (involving, for instance, nuclear collaboration) would be decisively influenced by what might appear to be political atmospherics.

Whether East-West or West-West, these problems, which have always existed, are obviously magnified by the widely analyzed change in values or priorities within developed liberal societies.

At a minimum, the decline of East-West confrontation and the emergence in each Western country (but particularly in the two crucial ones, the United States and West Germany) of new age or social groups with different formative experiences and interests and of newly acute domestic problems, challenge the role of defense, the primacy of foreign policy, and the ideological consensus on which the present system used to be based; they appear as new constraints that must be both fought and accommodated by the security system in order to fulfill the same function at lower cost and visibility.

At a maximum, these changes herald a more fundamental transformation in the relations of state (and of the interstate system) and society (domestic and transnational), in the role of military power and the meaning of security: from diplomacy and strategy to development and adaptation.

Obviously, the answer is complicated by the difference between "a less governmental West and the rest" (Hughes, 1972). As Francois Duchêne put it, the West (including the United States, if not the Nixon administration) may be reacting to the same challenges more as a society and the Soviet Union more as a state.

Perhaps, then, the fundamental issue is seen more clearly when looking beyond immediate East-West and United States-European issues, to their global context: are we at the beginning of a new international system and of a new international (or rather multinational) politics? If our conception of security and the organizations that are based on it were born of the needs of deterrence in an age of hostile bipolarity, should both the concept and the organization survive, disappear, or be adapted in an age of greater multipolarity, greater cooperation between former enemies, particularly between the two superpowers, and more civilian (if less civil) societies? Are these various directions (more multipolar, more cooperative, more domestic) compatible? Which should have priority?

The New International System and European Security

Seldom have abstruse and abstract notions about the nature of the international system been a theme for general political discussion as in the past two years. This is due mainly to America's current reassessment of its place in the world and to the Nixon Administration's flair for diplomatic initiatives and taste for theoretical rationalizations. The Nixon doctrine had indicated the general direction of a limited disengagement based on an ambiguous acknowledgment of the limits of American power and of international bipolarity. The Peking trip materialized the triangular character of the superpower game; together with the August 15, 1971 decisions, it may also be seen, in a sense, as the signal for the eventual emergence of a five-power world, by demonstrating—through a kind of American declaration of emancipation from its allies—the possible divergence of interests among the United States, Japan, and Western Europe.

The Moscow Summit, with the SALT agreements and the Soviet-American "Declaration on Basic Principles," closes the circle by showing that the news of bipolarity's death was vastly exaggerated: it had only undergone a conversion, from hostility to cooperation, from the struggle for supremacy to the joint management of world affairs.

At the same time, the Indo-Pakistani crisis showed the fallacy both of judging local situations primarily from the point of view of the global game between superpowers, and of assuming that the latter, particularly the Soviet Union, would necessarily exercise their influence on the side of restraint. Conversely, events in Vietnam and the Middle East, seen in connection with the Moscow Summit, have shown both how far in the new triangular situation the two Communist powers could go in giving precedence to their relations with the United States over their support of their allies, and how far smaller countries like North Vietnam and Egypt could go in refusing to comply with the conservative consensus at the top without, however, being able to break it.

Whatever else it is, then, the new international system is not simple. Two great roads seemed to open out of the hostile bipolarity of the Cold War. The first one is cooperative bipolarity. It consists of a reconciliation of the two camps, led by the two leaders, in the name of interdependence, convergence, and common interests—this could be called the Kennedy or the Monnet road. The second one is multipolarity—a new balance of power based on the reassertion of national interests and on the combinations of independent diplomacies; this could be called the Gaullist and, to some extent, the Nixon-Peking road. The first road could lead to new bipolar divisions: superpowers against middle and small powers, or developed north against under-developed south. The second road could lead to new conflicts, or at least unpredictabilities, between the participants in the new multipolar game, as well as to tensions between them (or the big-league players) and the others.

Obviously, today, we have elements of all these systems: the old East-West opposition, the new bipolar cleavages, and different types and levels of multipolarity—nuclear, economic, and political.

The simple view of a five-power balance has been torn into pieces by critics like Buchan, Brzezinski (1972), and Hoffman (1972), who have rightly shown the inequalities among the five and the multiplicity of types of power, and of cooperation, competition and conflict according to issue areas and to regions. Perhaps there was some overkill, since the formulations under attack were only indicating one of the directions of an American policy whose puzzling characteristic was precisely to operate at different places and times under different assumptions. This could come from day-to-day pragmatism disguised under successive and incompatible rationalizations; or it might reflect a more subtle and complex attempt at establishing a new, differentiated concert, meant to operate according to different rules and with different participants in different regions and on different issues, but with the United States always in a direct or indirect, single or joint, managing or balancing role.

The policy of the Nixon administration has been both more simple and more subtle, more brutal and more lucid about the links between different forms of power than its critics are willing to concede. For example, it is *not* true that the Nixon administration ignores the dimension of economic interdependence; it is true that it tries to use that dimension for accomplishing its own debatable political ends. All the achievements of the first Nixon administration can be interpreted as a skillful bargaining session, based on the application of one form of power (actual or potential) to compensate for another. Toward the Soviet Union, the United States has used economic and technological power (corresponding to the weaknesses and needs of its interlocutors) to extract military and diplomatic concessions (for example, on Vietnam). Conversely, toward Western Europe, which is strong economically but weak militarily and diplomatically, it uses the bargaining power of military protection for extracting economic concessions (or reasonable behavior). Diplomatically, it has used the opening to China to put pressure on Japan, the Soviet Union, and above all North Vietnam; and it may use its dialogue with the Soviet Union to put pressure not only again on North Vietnam but, in a different way, on Western Europe.

The real criticism, then, would be not that the Nixon administration ignores new realities, but that the way it handles them may produce dangerous results. As in the case of de Gaulle, ruthless acrobatics can win spectacular victories; they are less impressive as a foundation for a "stable structure of peace," especially if—as may be the case for President Nixon as opposed to his French counterpart—they are put in the service of narrow economic interests as much as of a broad political vision.

What matters for Europe is that, from each of these points of view, her situation becomes more ambiguous and potentially more uncomfortable, although she may yet turn ambiguity into opportunity and discomfort into challenge.

From the point of view of the persisting elements of Soviet-American bipolarity, the prevalent European impression is that the trend has been toward a shift in the military balance from American superiority to parity and, in some respects, Soviet superiority. This view arises either because the perception of Soviet regional superiority is no longer compensated by that of American strategic superiority, or even because some elements of the strategic equation itself—like the asymmetry in the number of offensive launchers allowed by the Moscow Interim Agreement, or the possibility that is left open to the Soviet Union to combine, in the future, MIRV technology with a greater number of launchers and heavier payloads—give to some, rightly or wrongly, the impression of present or future Soviet strategic superiority.

In relative dynamism and commitment, while both sides pursue an active diplomacy, the Soviets have been much more active in Europe. More generally, American initiatives are seen as brilliant tactical moves covering a strategic retreat, while the Soviet Union is not only much more engaged in Eastern Europe than the United States is in Western Europe, but is genuinely expanding its diplomatic influence and military presence in various areas. The Indian subcontinent is the most spectacular example; but her presence in the Mediterranean, her access to Middle East oil, and the successes of her German policy are no less important. In the last year, however, the Middle East has witnessed something of a turn of the tide. But it remains more generally true that, while both leaderships look to foreign policy successes as a compensation for domestic problems, international leadership is seen by important forces in American society as inimical to America's values and rightful priorities, while it may be indispensable to the legitimacy and authority of the Soviet regime.

Finally, the relationship between the two superpowers, while containing elements of conflict, of competition, and of cooperation, has taken a most important turn toward the latter with the Moscow Summit. The existence of a mutual interest of the superpowers in preventing nuclear war and in limiting the arms race has, of course, been widely recognized and welcomed by Europeans. Nevertheless, "contractualizing" this common interest and the cooperation designed to implement it (through such means as the creation of a bilateral standing consultative commission) has revived a feeling that was created by NPT but to date has remained low during the SALT negotiations. This feeling is a fear of "nuclear complicity" (as the former German Chancellor Kiesinger put it) or condominium.

Even more important, perhaps, the "Declaration of Basic Principles" suggests through much of its language that a "common strategic ideology" (Coral Bell) is emerging which is, for both, spilling over from strategy to politics. Some of the language of the Declaration, with restraint and peaceful coexistence replacing self-determination and socialism, and· with the "no unilateral advantage" formula, suggests a preference for the status quo over their respective objectives. The Vietnam context, the failure to mention any disagreement over the Middle East, the fact that on issues relevant for Europe (like MBFR and the

Security Conference) the American position either was held in reserve until, or was modified by, the summit meeting—all this suggests a primacy of cooperation between superpowers over their multilateral links with their respective allies.

Several years ago, Hedley Bull (1970) drew a series of useful distinctions among different types of superpower collaboration: a) joint management versus joint government; b) joint management limited to the control of nuclear weapons versus comprehensive joint management; c) twin or parallel hegemony versus joint hegemony; and d) de facto versus formally-agreed joint management. Looking at them today, one must admit that the Moscow Agreement represented in each of these cases a step beyond the first alternative in the direction of the second.

If one combines this impression with the earlier ones of Soviet strategic equality, local superiority, and stronger interest and commitment, one ends up with a condominium weighted on the Soviet side, at least as far as Europe is concerned.

There have been times when many Europeans have feared an excessive American superiority, excessive American involvement in their affairs, and dangerously hostile relations between the superpowers; today the predominant fears are in the opposite direction. The ideal superpower relationship from the point of view of Europe is an intermediary one: the United States sufficiently superior and sufficiently involved to protect Western Europe credibly and to marginally restrain the Soviet Union in marginal areas; and a superpower relationship of peaceful competition, equally removed from condominium and confrontation, thus giving third parties an importance and a role.

The loss of American superiority by itself would not have created a crisis of confidence; Europeans had lived under the assumption of qualitative U.S.-Soviet parity long before it was officially recognized. But parity plus disengagement (of troops or of attention) plus a changed relationship with the Soviet Union (namely, as Henry Kissinger put it: "a new relationship in which on both sides, whenever there is a danger of crisis, there will be enough people who have a commitment to constructive programs so that they could exercise a restraining influence") does raise the specter of a gap between U.S. and European perceptions of what constitutes dangerous or unacceptable Soviet behavior and what response, involving what risks, should be initiated to deter it. The divergence may be such as to give the Soviet Union a freedom of action (say, in Yugoslavia) comparable to that of the United States when it blockaded Haiphong. The Europeans would appear as weak, but immoral and malevolent spoilers of superpower harmony; they would have to convince themselves of the most reassuring interpretation of Soviet behavior, precisely because they would not be reassured.

The Changing Geometry of Power

It is too late, however, for a world jointly managed or governed by the two superpowers; the *triangular* aspect, perhaps overstressed at the time of the Peking visit, tends to be neglected after Nixon's visit to Moscow. Yet the first visit probably is one of the main keys to the success of the second. The existence of China does decisively influence Soviet attitudes toward the rest of the world and, conversely, the bargaining power of other parties toward the Soviet Union. Is this also the case for Europe? Should she look for a Chinese strategy, to balance the Soviet Union, or have the relations of the latter with both Europe and the United States become permanently peaceful because of the Chinese threat?

Again, much depends on how reassuring a view one takes of Soviet behavior. Regarding the influence of Moscow's preoccupation with China on her policies toward Europe, one can distinguish four interpretations of her priorities. From the most optimistic viewpoint, the Soviet Union wants peace and stability, détente, and disarmament (or at least force reductions) with the West because of her conflict with China.

From another perspective, the Chinese threat does constitute the main consideration, but this exactly leads the Soviet Union, given her definition of stability, to a more rigid and intransigent view of her rule in Eastern Europe and of her security toward the West: precisely because of China, she cannot afford to run any risk or suffer any diminution of power in Europe.

The third view—definitely a minority one, but defended by one of the most penetrating specialists, Michel Tatu (1972: 28-29)—reverses the first two. Tatu finds that periods of tension with China have not coincided with periods of détente with the West. The period of maximum tension with China (1963-1969) was also characterized by relatively rigid relations with the West. Since the end of 1969, the Soviet Union has sought a certain stabilization with China, in order to pursue a more active policy toward the West. The main thrust of her dynamism lies in expansion toward the west and the south, and particularly toward gaining decisive political influence on West European policies.

Finally, a fourth view (Valsalice, 1972: 43), which seems to the writer the most plausible one and is buttressed by impressive evidence, starts from the premises of the first two views, but reaches the conclusions of the third. The Soviet Union sees the conflict with China as her main problem, leading quite possibly to a major confrontation; but this impels for the Soviet Union an active policy of encircling China and of trying to control as much as possible the behavior of her potential partners, to encourage American withdrawal in order to become the center of a worldwide, anti-Chinese system. Just as the United States consciously or unconsciously used the containment of Russia to expand its presence and influence throughout the world in the late 1940s and the 1950s, Russia is on a course which she may see as defensive against China but which is as expansionist, if more realistic, as a revolutionary one.

Europe can see its role neither in encircling Russia with the help of China nor in becoming a passive instrument of the latter's encirclement by the former. Any thought of an active Chinese alliance aimed at putting pressure on Russia or on protecting Eastern Europe would only bring insecurity. On the other hand, Europe has a common interest with China in preventing the superpower condominium and, in particular, Soviet hegemony. Chinese interests in encouraging Western European unity and in establishing a certain presence in Eastern Europe coincide with the latter's interest in avoiding an exclusive tête-à-tête with the Soviet Union. Conversely, Europe has an interest not only in gaining some additional bargaining power in her détente dialogue, but also in the multilateralization of the nuclear dialogue and of arms control in general, hence in China's presence as well as in meeting the Chinese concern that the Security Conference and troop reductions in Europe should not be used as instruments to increase pressure on her.

The really difficult and obscure problems concern less the triangular aspect of world politics than its supposedly "pentagonal" one—with respect to the roles of Japan and Europe in the system. Here the doubts concerning the intentions of American policy in promoting the "five-power world" idea are matched only by the ambivalence of the Europeans themselves.

Can one be half a world power, or a second-class pole? Does the United States really want Western Europe and Japan to become full-fledged, militarily independent, hence nuclear, powers? Do Europe and Japan want it themselves? Would a pluralist Europe qualify? Would a five-power nuclear balance be more or less safe than a bi- or a tripolar one? On the other hand, does the evocation of the classical balance of power and its flexible alignments mean that the United States has no more permanent and intimate links with her allies than with her former opponents?

The suspicion is that the United States does not really expect or encourage a real five-power world from the nuclear point of view; but that it uses the idea both to justify a certain withdrawal of its protection, to encourage a greater effort from the Europeans (but in a framework defined by the triangular relationship), and to launch a tougher economic competition against them.

Critics like Brzezinski (1972) point out that, rather than one five-power world, one should consider two triangles: a strategic one (the United States, the Soviet Union, and China), and an economic one (the United States, Western Europe, and Japan) which is based on cooperation within the same system. But today, economic ties breed competition as much as cooperation. Indeed, once the ideological confrontation has abated, relations with opponents, especially nuclear ones, can be stablilized and basically cooperative; crises and conflicts are more likely to arise in relations with allies. The management of the Western capitalist system may be intrinsically more crisis-prone than that of nuclear deterrence: money may be harder to control than arms.

The same Europeans who have been criticizing the bipolar world now seem more worried by the danger of separation from the United States than flattered by their verbal promotion to the great power league. They fear that the old, U.S.-centered system may be receding more rapidly than their own ability to unite, their own willingness to make sacrifices and run risks for defense, and the constraints of the Soviet attitudes allow them to replace it.

Indeed, more than a time lag may be involved. Europe's and (in a different and ultimately lesser critical way) Japan's willingness and ability to play an independent great power role may be decisively affected by the new relations of state and society in the developed liberal world. She may be as affected as the United States by the combination of "neo-isolationism and neo-transnationalism" (Hughes, 1972), and in a more decisive way since she has an uphill battle for political unification and military power to wage.

Yet a certain West European consciousness is growing; the Common Market does exercise a powerful external influence. Diplomatically, the European scene has been transformed by the German-Soviet dialogue as much as the world scene by the U.S.–Chinese one. There is, then, a strong case for, and strong inclination toward, Western Europe and Japan specializing in the nonmilitary forms of power and becoming, in Francois Duchêne's expression, "the world's first civilian center of power."

The dilemmas of solidarity and flexibility, of power and dependence, and so forth, are insoluble for Europe in the framework of a world of threats, pressures, and conflict. They may be mitigated if the general framework is a cooperative one; if it is less that of a bipolar or of a multipolar balance of military power than that of a concert where different players make different contributions in different roles to the management of interdependence, whether in the arms control, the diplomatic, or the economic sphere.

Yet, while Europe has every interest in a general deemphasis of military power, being a civilian power in a world of military powers does not, when the chips are down, leave you with much civilian power either. Similarly, neither security nor independence may be fully accessible for anybody nor be the highest goal of politics; but a precondition for playing other roles is to be at least as secure or as independent as your partners in the concert.

Europe's political unity, economic power, or diplomatic influence are highly vulnerable as long as her security is entirely dependent upon American protection or Soviet good will. How to build up a third element of security that should mitigate the possible decline or unpleasant consequences of the other two without jeopardizing their existence; how to work both at improving and at deemphasizing the military balance; how to be in a position to choose détente and cooperation rather than being dragged into them by lack of choice: these are the ambiguous problems with which Europe is inevitably confronted by her ambiguous status.

The American side of this same dilemma has been well defined by Stanley Hoffmann (1972: 628-629):

> We are caught between our own desire for détente and the fear that it would be compromised if we build up those of our allies whom our adversaries most suspect. Our rivals' game is to improve their relations with us in so far as we tend toward disengagement without substitution—in which case, our self-restraint could benefit them.
>
> Two requirements for a new balance of power—relaxed relations with ex-enemies and greater power for ex-dependents—are in conflict. Such will be America's dilemma as long as our interest in "flexible alignments" is met by our rivals' search for clients.... Whether or not Western Europe and Japan become major actors, Eastern Europe and East or Southeast Asia will remain potential sources of instability.

No less important, then, than the problem of relations among the two, the three, and the five is that of the relations between this concert of great powers, whatever their number, and the rest of the world. By and large, Nixon, Brezhnev, Chou En-lai, and, one may add, Willy Brandt and Tanaka, have been quite successful in normalizing the relations between actual or potential great powers. What remains negative or in doubt is the impact on small and middle powers, whether within the spheres of influence of the great powers or in the Third World. The consequences of the Moscow Summit for the Middle East in particular are not yet clear. The tendency of the Nixon Administration and, in general, of great power diplomacy is to see in the planetary game the key to local situations. This has led to indisputable successes but also to indisputable failures, as in Bangladesh, which came from minimizing the autonomous role of social instabilities and national wills.

The highly ambiguous first two paragraphs of the Moscow Declaration are particularly striking in this respect. The first looks like an expression of the Soviet philosophy (including the notion of peaceful coexistence); and the second, the American one (emphasizing restraint, preventing situations capable of causing a dangerous exacerbation of their relations, and above all, renunciations of "efforts to obtain unilateral advantage at the expense of the other, directly or indirectly"), does seem to imply a primacy of great power interests over those of the local states or populations, especially if one remembers the absence of any reference to self-determination or to free movement. But any autonomous evolution in any country's social regime or diplomatic orientation can be interpreted as a direct or indirect unilateral advantage to one of the great powers. Does this give the other a green light for repression to reestablish the status quo, to establish an equivalent one or a claim to compensation?

Raymond Aron has remarked that the only way to implement the "no unilateral advantage" rule would be either a division into exclusive and intangible spheres of domination, or a mutual disengagement of the Great Powers from the rest of the world. In practice, two half-way houses are more likely. The first would be a combination of the two formulas (disengagment from disputed areas, but increased insistence on their own spheres). The second would mean, for disputed areas, a joint management or the working out of common solutions, by the Great Powers, in the tradition of nineteenth century conferences. Certainly for ambiguous regions, this is better than either unlimited competition or a passive backing of their respective allies by the Great Powers. But local conditions are likely to frustrate attempts at imposed solutions.

On the other hand, where one Great Power is clearly preponderant, an order based on domination rather than on consent is possible at the risk of explosions. This raises the crucial problem of whether the effect of multipolarization is going to be the multiplication of spheres of domination (each of the three or five dominating one region) and their consolidation (since they would no longer be challenged by a global ideological struggle); or whether it means a multiplication of opportunities for satellites or small allies to mitigate their subordination by increasing relations with outside powers without being accused of selling out to "the enemy," and a loosening of territorial and internal barriers through general interpenetration.

Military stability as such would seem to militate in the first direction, which clearly has the favor of the Soviet Union and an increasing degree of acquiescence of the United States. But, as Marshall Shulman and others have pointed out, the trends of modern society would seem to make a broader and more tolerant conception of security, based on nonintervention and free access, the only one compatible with peaceful change, which in turn is the only acceptable and, in the long run, the only accessible form of stability.

From this point of view, again, Europe is in a complex and ambiguous situation. Western Europe has neither the independence of the great powers, nor the forms of independence accessible to the Third World: geographical isolation; lack of attractive incentives for Great Powers presence; or the self-reliance and readiness to fight alone through political mobilization. She is too directly involved with the two superpowers, in interests and physical presence, to have the freedom of flexible alignments, yet too strong and domestically autonomous to be a simple satellite.

By contrast, Eastern Europe is the most directly-run sphere of domination in the world; yet that area is increasingly open to economic and, to some extent, human contact, which brings in return a tightening of central authority. Southern Europe is politically or socially unstable; parts of it, like Yugoslavia, are caught between the Soviet sphere of domination and a Third World situation. Local divisions and tensions make outside direct or indirect interference possible; national traditions make popular resistance likely. Those European areas that are domestically unstable and not tightly integrated in an alliance system share the dangers of other regions of the world with the difference that they are closer to the interests of the great powers and of their more stable neighbors.

A look at the complexities of the European map shows the impossibility of dividing it into two rigid spheres of influence; the Nordic balance is made of delicate shades going from the pro-Soviet neutrality of a Western-type society like Finland through the genuine neutrality of Sweden to Denmark's *sui generis* membership in NATO and the EEC, and Norway's in NATO alone. Yugoslavia is associated with both the EEC and Comecon; her social evolution draws her toward the West, her political difficulties bring her back closer to the East. The German Democratic Republic (GDR) is the champion of Eastern integration and of separation from the West, but it is also a member of the Common Market through the intra-German trade.

From the point of view of military security proper, the danger comes precisely from the ambiguity or the blurring of the lines that is encouraged and welcomed by modern social communication and by European political objectives. The logic of military security, as against that of the "no unilateral advantage" rule, would be a clear-cut separation either between the two Europes or between the European theater and the U.S.-U.S.S.R. strategic relationship. But West European interest in and influence on Eastern Europe, and Soviet interest in and influence on Western Europe, cannot help being part of the picture.

Similarly, the condition most favorable to a military freeze and eventual reduction of armed forces would be a freezing of the political status quo. The nightmare of planners in both alliances must be a crisis provoked by domestic evolution or revolution leading to changes in diplomatic alignment, even if they occur on the opposite side. Yet the forces for change cannot be permanently stifled, especially in the countries that combine a problem of personal succession. of political fragility of social tension, and of external vulnerability. They are, however, influenced by the external environment.

We are back, then, to the contradictions between the rigidities of the security system, the dynamics of social evolution, and the uncertain combinations of diplomatic objectives. To reconcile them means increasing the political confidence of Western Europe, caught between a cooler and less engaged United States and a stronger and more embracing Soviet Union; encouraging the limited political autonomy of Eastern Europe and its equally limited opening to the West by helping to make it safe for and from the Soviet Union; helping Northern and Southern Europe to overcome the dangers both of isolation and of unwanted interference, by protecting an exposed military situation in the north and an explosive national and social evolution in the south.

These policies would probably increase the overall security of the continent, including, ultimately, that of the superpowers. But they do correspond to given political objectives which may not be universally shared. They do raise questions of priority and of feasibility. They indicate a direction; they cannot provide a solution to the question of the relations between the general trends of the European situation and the objectives of the different powers.

European Priorities and Arms Control Objectives

In East-West relations in Europe, two main developments have been important: the political dialogue between West European countries and the East, and the strategic dialogue between the United States and the Soviet Union. In U.S.-West European relations, two dimensions have been dominant: the military ties and, increasingly, the economic strains; and, as we have seen, the two aspects are coming to be linked. But the nature of this link will be decisive for the security and the political future of Europe. They may become linked by an uncontrolled psychological process or by a deliberate political effort. The same applies, even more, to the relations between the two directions —East-West and West-West, as a whole—where a problem of compatibility and priority will increasingly arise involving the character, the orientation, and the role of the new Western Europe.

The Soviet Union has a clear interest in maintaining the distinction between her bilateral strategic dialogue with the United States and her continental dialogue with Western Europe; she has an even clearer interest in having both give priority to this dialogue with her over their dialogue with each other. Being a partner to both, she enjoys the advantage of unity, especially since her objectives in both relations are not so incompatible as to force her to embarrassing choices: her European policy no longer has the anti-German and anti-American emphasis characteristic of earlier periods. This is because, as we shall see in more detail in Part II, she seems to have solved, provisionally at least, her traditional double dilemma: priority to her rule in Eastern Europe versus increasing her influence in Western Europe, encouraging a "Gaullist" Europe without the United States versus maintaining a bipolar Europe run by the superpowers. Of course, this new approach entails risks to this very status quo, but the competition for mutual influence is not necessarily a loss for the Soviet Union, especially in the two Germanies and especially given the changing character of the American presence.

This is the key to the solution of the second dilemma. The Soviet Union no longer asks (or pretends to ask) for the dissolution of the blocs and the withdrawal of the United States. She wants, within the existing structures, to encourage a shift in the psychological balance, in the comparative unity and dynamism of the two superpowers, the two alliances, the two Europes, the two Germanies, the two Berlins. Her preferred solution is an American presence real enough to exercise some control over Germany and to prevent military efforts in Western Europe and false hopes in Eastern Europe, yet declining and uncertain enough to create doubts in West European countries—again, especially in Germany—and to prompt them to look for reassurance in accomodation to her.

As a minimum, the Soviet Union wants to discourage anything that might go against favorable existing trends and challenge the status quo by, for instance, creating a new center of power in Western Europe. She accepts the European economic integration, which may increase tension with the United States, but fights West European political and military unity which might deprive her of the fruits of these tensions. She probably sees European arms control as a way to decrease the American military presence while minimizing the risks of a West European military defense effort.

Negotiations conducted primarily with the United States and covering all nuclear weapons stationed in Europe would best serve this purpose. Alternatively, pan-European institutions negotiated primarily with the Europeans (where the United States and Canada would be present, but might increasingly appear as marginal participants or tolerated guests) could also serve as vehicles to protest against the organization of a European defense.

Today it is the United States, much more than the Soviet Union, that is faced with a conflict of priorities. The détente, domestic, economic, and psychological pressures, the ending of the draft, nuclear parity producing increasing reluctance to face the remaining risks of escalation to strategic war, the sheer wastefulness and irrationality of the present number and deployment of tactical nuclear weapons in Europe—all this makes some change in American posture and doctrine highly likely in the coming years. Even if the decision and moves were in fact unilateral, some kind of negotiated framework or fig leaf would be almost indispensable. The question is whether this negotiation should take place primarily with America's allies or with the Soviet Union.

At a time when the Soviet Union appears as a forthcoming arms control partner, the Common Market appears as an irritating economic competitor and a political/military Europe as "a dream, and not even a beautiful one," the case for superpower bilateralism has never been stronger.

In arms control, SALT I, SALT II, and MBFR would form a continuum. After having straightened out their strategic nuclear relationship, the United States and the Soviet Union may well resolve their tactical nuclear one. After a start on the risks of strategic instability and the control of the arms race, they would place an emphasis (already indicated in the "Basic Principles") on the risks of escalation and on the control of those allied forces that might contribute to it. The removal of FBS through SALT II or MBFR would give both a physical and an official sanction to the distinction, which already exists in practice, between Eastern Europe and the Soviet Union. It would mean acceptance of the Soviet (and increasingly, American) definition of "strategic", hence of the "sanctuarization" of the territories of both superpowers. A non-transfer clause for offensive missiles, on the model of the one on ABM, would also not only physically hamper the prospects of a new U.S.-European collaboration on defense, but do it in a way that would be symbolic of the primacy of U.S.-U.S.S.R. ties. Finally, mutual troop reductions arrived at in this context would also be symbolic of the new status of a "decoupled" Europe, especially if they were not accompanied by collateral measures designed to protect the interests of smaller allies or of outside powers.

From the arms control decoupling of SALT, one would arrive both at the political decoupling of U.S.-U.S.S.R. relations from the evolution of Europe and at the military decoupling of the strategic balance from the European theater.

Many features of present American practice and doctrine (see Secretary Laird's use of the distinctions between "theater" and "strategic" in his FY 1972 annual statement) point toward the direction just outlined, although other indicators suggest an opposite trend—such as the concept of "total forces" and the more favorable attitude it implies toward the French and British nuclear forces. Many more proposals currently being discussed (for the complete removal or for the redeployment of tactical nuclear weapons, for a "no-first-use of nuclear weapons" declaration, and so on) seem to originate in arms control circles but to carry the same political implications.

As for the U.S.-West European relationships, bilateralism has its own temptations. The old trade-offs among economics, politics, and security (the United States accepting short-term economic disadvantages for the long-term political advantages of European integration, Europe accepting the primacy of the dollar because of the protection of American troops, and so forth) are functioning less and less well. The United States is subjected to domestic pressures both toward vigorous intervention to protect what it feels as a threat to its growing economic interests in Europe, and toward military disengagement from a pacified and ungrateful continent. This paradox of increasing economic and decreasing military involvement can be resolved in three different ways: (a) through a static equilibrium, each dimension setting limits to the other; (b) through progressive substitution, the special U.S.-European relationship being maintained but on a more and more economic and less and less military basis —investments replacing soldiers as tokens of engagement; (c) through escalation—economic interdependence being conducive to conflicts and these tending to have a fall-out on military relations that would be used as means of pressure or would bear the brunt of the mutual bitterness leading to disengagement. Precisely for this reason, there is an appeal to playing upon special relationships with different partners in order to maintain a central position.

The case for American unilateralism or bilateralism against the primacy of the alliance or the encouragement of an emerging Europe would be unanswerable if either the United States could maintain its global or central position in the world's different functional or regional systems, or if it could withdraw into isolation either because other great powers were doing the same or because it had no serious interest in the structure of the world it left behind. But if it is true both that domestic pressures and international trends make a certain American retreat, disengagement, decommitment, decoupling, "lowering of the posture," and so on, necessary or desirable, and yet that the world is still an interdependent and unequal one in which power has to balance power and peace has to be managed, then there is no substitute for devolution, rebalancing, and regionalization.

Even in economic transatlantic relations, it may be that the central role of the United States is no longer in its interest or within its reach. For instance, the monetary system while remaining a common one may have to turn from a U.S.-centered into a bipolar or pluralistic one, for which the emergence of a European monetary block, zone, or policy—however annoying in the short run—is a necessary condition.

In security, the "Nixon doctrine"—while disastrous if translated mechanically into Vietnamization or Europeanization—nevertheless contains inescapable logic. A diminution in America's role may be caused by domestic forces and justified by changes in her perception of her rival; it must, unless these changes are so radical that not only the threat of these rivals but also their power have disappeared, be supplemented or substituted by regional forces. A universalistic management of the world (universal, joint, or parallel) could be the basis of an intransigent nonproliferation policy. In a more complex world where a less powerful and global America cannot offer the same protection, she obviously must accept the risk that smaller potential or actual nuclear countries rely on their own forces, whatever they are worth. If she wants to prevent them or to channel their efforts in the least dangerous directions, she must rely on a differentiated regional "proliferation-limiting" policy based on alliances, rather than on a universalistic "nonproliferation" policy based on condominium.

In Europe, a decoupling strategy aimed at removing any risk of escalation from local to strategic war would ruin the very basis of deterrence as it is now seen, at least by the Europeans. It is true that today, already, "the implications of U.S.-U.S.S.R. parity for nuclear deterrence in Europe" are such that "the U.S.-U.S.S.R. strategic nuclear force relationship compensates less now than ever for such local European imbalances as might develop." (The quotations here are from Ellsworth, 1972: 147.) And "it is plain—both from the U.S.-U.S.S.R. balance and from the way we have structured our forces that the United States has two concurrent strategies of deterrence: one strategy for prevention of political coercion or military attack on the United States itself, and one strategy for prevention of coercion or attack on NATO Europe." But it is also plain today that nuclear deterrence

> rests not on a nuclear threat but on a seamless web of deterrent systems ranging from the professional infantry man, through tactical and theatre nuclear forces actually located in Europe, up to sea-based and U.S. land-based missiles. And it is plain that the deterrence provided by these military systems rests ultimately on political solidarity, and unity of political-military intention. One

> principal effect of deterrence is uncertainty. The political-military
> intention is to prevent war or coercion in Europe by preventing the
> Warsaw Pact's military planners being able to assure their political
> authorities (or even themselves) what the response would be in case
> of an incursion into Western Europe [Ellsworth, 1972: 147].

The "unity of political-military intention" may already be a myth; but it too partakes of the ambiguity and the uncertainty on which deterrence is based.

This is in line with the formulation proposed by Timothy Stanley: "assured response and flexible escalation." In other words, one knows there would be an American response and one cannot be sure what it would be or, at least, how far it would go or what it would lead to. There is a wide consensus among Europeans on the notion that the risk of escalation is today the central element of deterrence in Europe, as opposed to either conventional response or massive retaliation; that it has greater credibility than either; and that it is less sensitive to differences in strength. The basis of deterrence is less the credibility of a deliberate decision than the unpredictability of a process; the substitute for American strategic *superiority,* which gave its plausibility to the former concept, is *continuity* between the two American-led systems of deterrence. The instruments of this continuity are American troops and theater nuclear systems based on the continent of Europe and, more generally, the "seamless web" constituted by the overlapping character of weapon systems.

This continuity would be broken by "putting the deterrent at sea," or eliminating weapon systems on grounds of their vulnerability or because they may reach the Soviet Union. Certainly, as long as no gap in this continuity of deterrence is created, there is nothing wrong with modernizing our military posture by eliminating costly, militarily useless, and vulnerable systems. But one should not forget that the search for eliminating any risk and any irrationality, characteristic of American arms controllers, may be doubly self-defeating. It is arguable that by removing what Bernard Brodie has called "the de-escalating effect of the threat of escalation," one makes escalation less unlikely; by removing uncertainty about escalation, one may be removing the certainty of nonaggression, since the European theater becomes a conventional one among others, subject to the same uncertainties as in other times and continents. One would certainly create political uncertainty among European allies. They would seek reassurance either in their own accommodation with the Soviet Union (a likely consequence of any bilateral disengagement which, for reasons of geography and ideology, would necessarily be asymmetrical) or in trying to recreate uncertainty by a nuclear strategy. Certainly, faced with a combination of U.S.-U.S.S.R. strategic parity, removal of tactical nuclear weapons, and reductions of American conventional forces, their reaction would not be to reestablish a conventional balance by themselves.

The only way to make European reactions to U.S. military changes and arms control agreements compatible with U.S. and arms control interests, is to make these changes and agreements compatible with European perceptions of their security and interests to begin with. And the only way to achieve that is by putting them in the framework of a new transatlantic discussion, possibly involving a new relationship between American and allied nuclear efforts—strategic and tactical, a new conventional strategy, a new negotiation either of NATO or of relations between the United States and the four European middle powers. But this obviously involves a minimum of agreement among Europeans themselves.

For military and arms control measures, as well as for pan-European security talks and for economic and monetary matters, an intra-Western dialogue is an urgent prerequisite to the East-West dialogue, and an intra-West European community agreement or at least convergence is a prerequisite for a fruitful dialogue with the United States. But isn't this West European element always going to be the missing link in these various dialogues? Do the West Europeans themselves agree on this order of priorities between negotiations among themselves, with the United States, and with the East?

The answer has to be cautious and tentative, but less negative than in other periods. While the period 1963-1968 were the years of maximum divergence, the pivotal years 1969-1972 are beginning to produce a certain convergence of attitudes toward the outside world. This is reflected at the level of personalities (compare the relations among Mr. Wilson, General de Gaulle, and Chancellor Erhard with those among Mr. Heath, Mr. Pompidou, and Mr. Brandt) and at the level of institutions. While one cannot speak of a common European policy toward the East, much less toward monetary and economic relations with the United States and even less toward military affairs because of the French absence from NATO, it is nevertheless true that the Nine have made more progress toward concerting policies on the security conference and presenting a common front in Helsinki, the meetings of ministers of the community have made more progress on monetary issues, and the Eurogroup on common projects and points of view in defense and U.S.-European issues than skeptics had expected.

These are only timid beginnings. Divergent domestic evolutions (dramatized by social conflict and by crucial elections) can challenge them at any moment. On the other hand, even if the progress we expect in the coming years does materialize, the harder options would come even later. Especially if the external environment presents unpleasant or dramatic alternatives, the priorities of key West European countries may well be shown to differ. Meanwhile, in spite of many nuances and inconsistencies, a common West European consciousness and an emphasis on West European priorities are on the increase.

They are fed above all, it would seem, by a new feeling of West European loneliness. This comes from a certain sobering of expectations or cooling of excitement toward the East after the successive French and German euphorias, after the discovery of certain diverging interests with the United States, after the August 1971 shock, and from a certain feeling of helplessness or passivity in light of the superpower dialogue after the Moscow meeting.

With the East, after the Gaullist preface and the German normalization, what is left to do seems either very long-range (the process of reconciliation, interpenetration, and mutual influence possibly leading to structural changes beyond our control) or fairly marginal (electoral benefits at home, increase in economic trade and cooperation, discreet attempts to improve the freedom of movement of persons and ideas between East and West without angering Eastern European governments, and the freedom of action of these governments without angering the Soviet Union).

The French know that Europe from the Atlantic to the Urals has been postponed for the foreseeable future after the Prague invasion; indeed, they have come to fear a Europe from the Urals to the Atlantic. French authorities point to the growth of Soviet power, to the necessity not to hamper the military balance through MBFR, to the desirability of increasing defense budgets.

In the case of German policy toward the East, after the signature of the various treaties, faith in history takes the place of practical bargaining, particularly since the attempts at influencing the evolution of the East German regime have, so far, been successfully resisted by the latter's policy of *Abgrenzung*. The West German government has all the more reason to moderate the hopes of its population and to find other policy goals since the need of practicing a certain ideological *Abgrenzung* itself is made even more obvious by the atmosphere in academic and "young Socialist" circles.

Both France and Germany, moreover, cannot help feeling that the happy days when they enjoyed the initiative in détente and were the subjects of the curiosity and worries of their allies are superseded, as soon as the subject is military, by a return to the old situation. As in the Kennedy or the NPT days, it is the United States who deals with Moscow and reassures its allies that they are not being forgotten or betrayed. Some, in Bonn or Paris, would like to recapture the initiative and beat the United States to Moscow bilaterally within MBFR or within the context of the CSCE, which they see as a "second pillar of SALT." In particular, the strategy of the German government has often tried to anticipate dangerous American trends by preempting them, or at least by trying to influence and channel them by making their own proposals in the same direction. Examples include Germany's concept of MBFR, seen as a process involving indigenous forces, or her attempt to influence the discussions of SALT and the sensitive issues of forward-based systems by putting forth her own ideas about the reduction of tactical nuclear weapons. But the prevalent interest, for the time being, is more on the new Paris-London-Bonn triangle and on the old problem of the character of relations among Western European countries and between them and the United States.

The "Struggle for Britain"

Indeed, we are back to the issues of 1962-1963 (Fouchet Plan, British entry, Partnership, Kennedy Round), with important changes in the situation and disposition of all parties involved. The most obvious difference is that now Britain is in the Common Market and her relations with France are good. If East-West relations in Europe can ultimately be seen as an episode in the historic "struggle for Germany," American-West European relations can, in a way, be described as a "struggle for Britain." Only Britain can lead the way out of the sterile opposition between a "European" and an "Atlanticist" Europe toward a progressively more independent Europe in conjunction with the United States.

Britain's new attitudes toward the Common Market and its more general new unpredictability have shown to even the most Atlanticist Europeans that in some respects the European construction, if it is to progress, must do so not necessarily against the United States but very possibly against its opposition or objections. On the other hand, while the logic of American leadership under Kennedy and strategy under McNamara were hostile to European military independence and to British-French nuclear collaboration, the logic of the Nixon doctrine and of Henry Kissinger's ideas is more ambiguous; so are the messages issued by the American administration. By and large, as Jean Laloy points out, while the Soviet Union opposes Europe's economic integration less than her political-military union, the United States has increasing objections toward the former and decreasing ones against the latter. The course that Europe will be able to steer among these obstacles and incentives will obviously depend both on the respective priorities of her major countries and on the evolution of their common situation.

For the time being, France has been maintaining almost completely contradictory positions. She wants to keep the American military presence, but wants to do nothing—either in terms of specific contributions or of general policy—to help prevent or slow down the disengagement she fears. She has, until recently, reached complete economic and monetary independence from the United States and blamed her European partners for not sufficiently sharing this attitude; yet she does nothing to help provide an alternative to the security link which limits the possibility of European independence by giving the United States a decisive leverage, especially toward Germany. Being reluctant to speak either about European defense or about European arms control, France has seemed to be entirely conservative in military matters and revolutionary in economic relationships, at least openly and at least until very recently, at finding a compromise between the two.

Germany, by contrast, professes to see no conflict between being wholeheartedly attached to European integration, to the Atlantic alliance, and to détente with the East. She is second to none in the first direction, but is likely to be more sensitive than most to American and Soviet objections against Europe's economic or military course. While prominent in Eurogroup activities, she is also among the most sensitive to domestic pressures against defense, and tends to prefer the MBFR route to the European defense one as a means of preventing American troop reductions or compensating for them if they do occur.

Britain, at least under Edward Heath, seems to have the clearest set of priorities: Western over pan-European attaching an increasing importance to the European link as compared to the Atlantic one, but without prematurely compromising the latter.

The countries on the northern and southern flanks of the Atlantic alliance have a primary interest both in the maintenance of the American presence, which is their unifying link with the center, and in détente and arms control to the extent that they diminish the dangers of their exposed position. To the extent that the American presence is weakening, their main concern is to avoid isolation through a regionalization of the Central European defense. Their link with the EEC would, then, become increasingly important for their security.

Finally, Eastern European countries know, especially since the treaties with Germany, that their only security problem is with the Soviet Union. They would welcome arms control measures that might marginally make Soviet intervention more awkward and security talks or institutions within which they would be less confined to a tête-à-tête with their leader than in real life. Beyond that, they know that Western Europe, especially Germany, has a greater interest in interpenetration versus the political status quo than the United States, and they welcome an active West European Ostpolitik. They are favorable to West European integration if it encourages it, hostile if it deflects from it. They are interested in avoiding a Soviet superiority over the continent, which would increase their dependence. In a situation of balance, some indirect and marginal deterrence through uncertainty may still be available, at least to some of them. Hence they are interested in keeping the American presence, or *faute de mieux* in the creation of a European balance to replace it, although they would, of course, never imitate the Chinese in saying so officially.

Nobody, perhaps not even the Soviet Union, has an interest in forcing abrupt choice among the Atlantic, the West European, and the East-West direction. Everybody has an interest in the continuation of the American presence, in the progress of détente, and in the growth of a West European role of responsibility and initiative. In the long run, the desirable sequence would be from East-West (i.e. above all American-Soviet and German-Soviet) stabilization, through growing West European unity and influence and through East European autonomy and Soviet tolerance based on domestic transformation, toward a new multilateral system of balance and cooperation which would de-emphasize both the presence of the superpowers and the role of military force.

Unfortunately, however, the dynamics of Europe's security problem originate much less, today, in the progress of either West European integration or pan-European cooperation than in the trends toward American disengagement or decoupling, which revive the old European fears of the late 1940s and early 1950s ("we want to be defended, not liberated") and of the 1960s ("we want deterrence, not defense, because any war on the European soil would be disastrous").

Today, there is no denying that Europe's security is increasingly distinct from, and inferior to, that of the United States. Europe sits between the two stools of complete Atlanticism (which would mean the complete identification of her territory with that of the United States—as voiced in Kennedy's Berlin statement—and the meeting of any threat to her security with the same threat of retaliation against the Soviet Union as a threat to the U.S. would invoke—again, as expressed in Kennedy's Cuban missile crisis statement) and complete Europeanism (which would mean having for herself this ability to credibly threaten retaliation against the Soviet Union).

Europe's present security—inferior but acceptable—rests on ambiguous deterrence and uncertain escalation coupled with East-West détente; and as we have seen, continuity with the U.S. strategic deterrence is the substitute, in terms of protection, for U.S. strategic bipolarity. If it is put into question, Europe thus becomes either a zone of potential conventional conflict (the Gaullist nightmare of the two superpowers sparing each other's territory and fighting, directly or indirectly, over Western and Eastern Europe) or a militarily passive, quasi-neutralized zone of reduced armaments supervised by the superpowers.

To avoid these two unpleasant situations, she must try to maintain all three elements of her present security, while changing their respective proportion in the light of circumstances. After all, if Europe—in spite of the most unnatural territorial divisions and the starkest ideological oppositions—has not known the equivalent of the Korean, the Vietnam, the Arab-Israeli, or the Indo-Pakistani war, it can be only for three reasons: the direct physical presence of the superpowers, the presence of nuclear weapons, and the more peaceful or satisfied character of her societies. Each of these three features, if taken in isolation, would be inaccessible, insufficient, or dangerous.

The first would mean perpetuation of the division of Europe, complete renunciation of an independent Western Europe, and a degree of identification with the United States—which trends in the latter would no longer permit, even if the Europeans wanted it.

Trying to substitute European nuclear deterrence for the

American umbrella would, if it meant a full-fledged European deterrent, be conceivable only in case of dire need, if the feeling of abandonment by the United States and of threat by the Soviet Union were sufficient to overcome the internal resistance to political unity and defense expenditure. As Ian Smart (1972: 197-198) has remarked, the very conditions that would create the new separation from the United States and hostility from the Soviet Union would be worsened, at least in the short run, by the solution and, at any rate, make its implementation more difficult.

Finally, banking on the obsolescence of military balance considerations and deterrence—through collective security, the dissolution of blocs, European reconciliation, or the primacy of civilian values—would ignore both the structural problems created by the predominance of actual Soviet and potential German power on the European continent, the potential for violent crises in developed societies, and the nature of domestic and interstate relationships in the Soviet world.

There are no alternatives, then, from the point of view of security itself, to:

(1) Keeping much of the present deterrence and defense structure intact for as long as possible: This means that the United States ought not to remove essential features of the present structure nor underline its weaknesses in the name of détente or of arms control. For the Europeans, this means contributing more actively (financially and by their general policy) to prolongation of the present structure.

(2) Progressively, under the umbrella of the present structure, reinforcing the European elements and their coordination with the corresponding U.S. forces: This means that the Europeans ought not to match eventual U.S. troop reductions by reductions of their own. Europe must take steps toward a conventional defense community, adding an element of "uncertainty of non-escalation" by the deployment of British and French tactical nuclear weapons, in coordination with American ones, and proceed toward the coordination of French and British nuclear forces and the creation of a European NPG, provided it is made

compatible with a restructured Atlantic alliance. For the Americans, this policy means opening a serious process of discussion with European allies about possible changes in NATO strategy prompted by reduced U.S. troop levels (for different possible models, see Hunt, 1973; Nehrlich, 1973). It means that the United States must accept the need for a dialogue about, and possibly coordination with and help for, European nuclear efforts, tactical and strategic, if and when the Europeans, including the French, show a real interest in practical cooperation and structural reform.

(3) Pursuing an active policy of détente, cooperation, and interpenetration toward Eastern Europe, while knowing that its limits are near and its fruits are distant. It would be desirable to emphasize nonmilitary aspects, such as economic and cultural contacts, and the political guarantees of their regular course. Within political and military relations, the aspects to be emphasized are nonintervention, crisis-management, verification, and codes of conduct—all the kit of collateral "confidence-building" or rather "confidence-substituting" measures, rather than arms limitations and changes in the security structure of Europe. These should be involved in the last stage of European reconciliation, not in the first. Meanwhile, the discussion around the conference on security and cooperation and the institution of standing pan-European commissions should be considered as positive channels for a peaceful transformation of the continent as long as they do not interfere with the process of West European integration and with the theoretical possibility of its political and military consequences, which should have priority. Indeed, it is only if West Europeans are confident in their resolve to progress toward unity that they can and should run the risks of interpenetration and favor institutions that present dangers but also opportunities.

The Conference on Security and Cooperation in Europe may be limited to blessing the status quo through one or several spectacular meetings. At the other extreme, it may give rise to a complete pan-European organization—economic, cultural, military, and so on—that would tend to replace or supersede existing organizations or, conversely, to force neutral, nonaligned or heretical states to become more integrated into them because of their added pan-European legitimacy. According to a third and more positive view—precisely because, on tangible matters of security and economy, existing organizations would maintain and develop their role of threatening the independence of states and consolidating the division of Europe—an open and institutionalized political dialogue would be useful, as long as it were based on the mutual acceptance of interpenetration and of common rules regulating it.

In principle, this could also apply to arms control, as long as all parties remember that there is no positive value to arms limitations as such, divorced from their political context. Arms control, in the most general sense, does have two basic universal goals that are positive by themselves: the avoidance of war and the limitation or decrease of defense expenditures. But as soon as one asks "what war?" and "what expenditures?" and "negotiated by whom?"—one enters into the decisive political questions of relations between superpowers, alliance systems, and individual small and middle powers. Arms control can be an excellent bureaucratic ideology, used to manipulate wrong-headed military services or obnoxious allies into submission; it can also be used by smaller allies to limit the control of their leaders.

MBFR—to take the most salient European example—can be seen as an anti-Mansfield device or as the continuation of Mansfield by other means. It can be seen, as by the French government, as a way for the alliance leaders to reassert their control or, as seen by the German government, as a way for alliance members to have a voice in a process that, if it did not take place on a multilateral basis, would still proceed on a unilateral or bilateral one. Or it can be interpreted as a way of undermining "the blocs" by delineating the beginnings of an alternative security system.

Similarly, in the East, MBFR can be viewed as a pro-Warsaw Pact device entirely controlled by the Soviet Union, or as a way for individual countries to get—through collateral measures—some of the security that already exists between alliances: essentially, an "anti-Prague invasion" device.

Finally, from the point of view of noncentral regions, MBFR

can increase their exposed situation, if it is limited to central Europe, or it can connect the three security zones and thereby reemphasize the notion of the indivisibility of peace in Europe.

In our own view, the issues of participation and priorities are essential. CSCE and SALT will proceed and possibly with good results—provided the marginalization of American participation in pan-European institutions is avoided in the first, and provided SALT is Europeanized when talking about matters involving Europe. European nuclear powers should be present in its standing consultative commission, as a step toward a long-range multilateralization of SALT to include all nuclear powers.

MBFR, apparently the exercise most favorable to the West, may be the most ambiguous one. It may come too late or be too slow to forestall or slow down domestic American pressures for unilateral reduction; and it may come too early for a new security system to be developed. Its value and its danger for security are more indirect than direct. They are linked above all to the questions of who will take part in the negotiations and who will take part in the reductions. It would seem that the preferred solution, for the United States, would be bilateral reductions bilaterally arrived at; and for the Federal Republic, multilateral reductions multilaterally arrived at. This writer would share the British preference for bilateral reductions multilaterally arrived at (i.e., for reductions limited to the superpowers, but with negotiations involving the small and middle powers). But I fear that in reality the opposite may happen: that multilateral reductions will be bilaterally arrived at, and that the real negotiation would be restricted to the superpowers. Yet such a process would start a sequence of general reduction, entailing the danger of a militarily neutralized and politically "Finlandized" Europe.

The positive value of MBFR and of the whole negotiating process lies not in dismantling a relatively safe military balance for which there is no substitute in sight, but in changing the character of political relations. It will have been worth the trouble and the risks if, by becoming a permanent feature of the process of East-West communication, it contributes, directly or indirectly, to modifying the behavior of its participants in the direction of restraint. For, more than mutually balanced force reductions, what European security needs is a process of mutually balanced interpenetration and nonintervention, and a mutually balanced reduction in the role of force.

PART II.

Facing East:
A "Normalized" Europe?

A fter the tanks in Prague came the talks in Helsinki. The city of the Wall is also the city of the four-power agreement and of the treaty between the two German states. Presidents and businessmen travel back and forth between Moscow and Western capitals; Czech intellectuals and Soviet dissidents travel only to mental wards or to exile. Occasionally, the testimony of an expelled critic or a message from Prague tell a not-too-interested Western public about the other side of détente.

Has Eastern Europe grown closer or more distant? Indeed, did it or will it ever really attract the attention of the West, whether in terms of moral or ideological solidarity or in terms of security and power?

The invasion of Czechoslovakia did not produce a serious risk of war, nor did it compromise the circumstances of détente, though it did modify the nature of it profoundly. The Prague Spring and then its suppression raised many deep problems in a deeply moving way: the reciprocal discovery and subsequent dialogue between people and leaders; the problem of resistance and violence in a highly developed society; the question of the compatibility of socialism and freedom or, on the other hand, of socialism and imperial domination. Nevertheless, how many West Europeans saw these vital problems in a new light because of Czechoslovakia? By way of contrast, how many people think that Eastern Europe is uninteresting because revolution to their minds can only be romantic and violent, imperialism can only be capitalist, or socialism tyrannical? Too far away to concern us, too near to fascinate, Eastern Europe has no luck with its Western neighbors, even on the moral and ideological level.

This is even truer on the level of power relations. Left-wing intellectuals are tempted to neglect it because it disturbs their moral comfort; right-wing governments neglect it (except at election time) because it disturbs their diplomatic comfort. Till very recently, whoever talked of Soviet imperialism in Eastern Europe was automatically suspected of stirring up the Cold War on behalf of American imperialism. Nowadays, one could only be accused of being an agent of Peking, since China is the only power that explicitly and actively questions the legitimacy of the Soviet empire. Meanwhile, the United States, acting within the framework of summit agreements (symbolized by the meeting in Moscow at the time of the Haiphong blockade), and Western Europe, acting within the framework of different bilateral dialogues and the multilateral one on European security, are both in the process of granting the Soviet Union the formal consecration of its sphere of domination which it has sought for twenty-five years. At the very time that it is losing the authority of ideological leadership, Soviet domination is still winning by the evidence of its military authority.

In the short term, the dangerous or interesting regions are those that are contested or ambiguous. These are regions where the great powers are present, though one does not know the extent of their commitment or their powers of control: Asia and the Near East. The massive and determined nature of the Soviet presence in Eastern Europe harms the universal attraction of communism. But it intimidates those in the West who are impressed by force and reassures those who are frightened by instability. The declining solidarity of the revolutionary International is offset by the growing solidarity of the conservative Holy Alliance.

The question at the moment, which has a significance beyond the bounds of Eastern Europe, is whether the alliance of an imperial ideology and a military balance, both equally rigid, is sufficient to guarantee the sealing off of a region—when it is opposed not only by the local people's aspirations to national independence and their desire to communicate with the outside world, but also by the tendencies of modern societies, economics, and technology toward interpenetration. Should one have more confidence in impersonal forces than in the will of men? Will Eastern Europe, cast yet again in role of an object rather than a subject, be swept along like all other "preserves" by the dynamics of a more general evolution?

The Consecration of Yalta

When seen from Western Europe, this tendency to wager on an historic evolution of a global nature rather than on a specific political endeavor appears doubly tempting, because it is based on a great number of objective precedents as well as on the hierarchy of Western interests. Eastern Europe has had its own national revolutions and social upheavals. However, throughout history its fate has been decided at least as much by the outcome of some more generalized situation or evolution, whose main determining factor was the respective situations and the mutual relations of the great powers surrounding it. In retrospect, for example, the period between the two wars—the era of balkanization and of relative freedom of action between several influences—now appears as an interregnum, brought about by specific circumstances (the eclipse of Russia and Turkey), which was then suppressed by Russia's reappearance on the scene.

As far as Russia is concerned, Eastern Europe constitutes an immediate interest of intrinsic value and is essential to what remains in the way of imperial authority, both from the point of view of ideology and of actual power. But what is it for the others? For the United States, and nowadays for China, it is part of the global tug-of-war that either throws them into opposition or binds them to the Soviet Union. To China, it is an essential factor in a double sense: apart from the conflict of powers, there is the ideological rivalry of two forms of communism and the fact, rooted in geography, that the more secure Russia feels about her empire in the West, the more threatening she may look in the East. But to the United States, Eastern Europe is a factor of marginal importance, which has never been either formally conceded to or energetically disputed with the Soviet Union.

The Cold War was not a result of any dividing up of the world into spheres of influence, nor an active struggle to gain power over such spheres, but it was rather a stalemate, a kind of static or trench warfare, with each of the great powers knowing that it had no direct access to one half of Europe, yet doing everything possible to make its digestion difficult for the opponent. It has always been the Soviet Union and Western Europe, in particular Germany, which counted for the United States; showing an interest in Eastern Europe meant above all creating difficulties for the Soviet Union and keeping open the possibility of German reunification. In both cases, the attitude was kept up without much energy or conviction. From the moment that détente with the Soviet Union and the division of Germany were accepted, the earlier attitude seemed in the process of being abandoned almost with relief.

From now on, this existing division (which was provisionally accepted as a lesser evil) is gradually being replaced by a rightful division, seen as one of the elements of the new American-Soviet cooperation and considered essential to the new world order. With this shift from conflict to cooperation of the great powers, the Yalta agreement on spheres of influence is gradually losing its mythical character and is becoming reality. Once again, then, the East Europeans can only work out the consequences of a development that is beyond their control.

Apart from the Germans, the West Europeans determine their attitude to Eastern Europe mostly in relation to the organization of Western Europe itself and its relations with the United States and the Soviet Union. When people emphasize the "building" of Europe, they are thinking, above all, of Western Europe. When people stress détente, it is primarily the Soviet Union they are thinking of. In Western discussion on the nature of transatlantic or East-West relations, Eastern Europe is raised only as a minor argument to prove that the Soviet danger still exists or, on the contrary, to show the transformation of communism. For West Europeans, the Europe of prosperity and, to a great extent, of freedom, is Atlantic Europe or at least the Europe of the

American challenge. For a declining but still substantial number, the Europe of ideology is represented by the Soviet Union; so is, for an increasing number, the Europe of power.

Among these perspectives, what picture of Europe could Westerners have which would emphasize their links with their Eastern neighbors, who are neither prosperous nor powerful? Ideally, one can only see two possibilities in international structure: a Europe of small and medium powers, whether a Europe of independent nations standing up to the great powers, or Europe as a third force. In ideology, Europe is invoked as a third way: as a synthesis of capitalism and socialism; or, alternatively, it could refuse both and aim at an original model—thus constituting a European model of both civilization and social organization.

Considering these two points of view, perhaps a European who belongs to both the East and the West will be forgiven when he is occasionally tempted to say: "If Eastern Europe only could! If Western Europe only would! " It is a fact that, confronted by (and perhaps because of) obstacles and risks to a far greater extent than in the West, the experience of one East European country provides a remarkable example of great perseverance in quest of independence, while the experience of another, like the Prague Spring, reveals a serious and precise awareness of the ills both of communism and capitalism, suggesting, if not the means, at least the direction by which one might transcend them. Finally all these countries, when given a chance, show an awareness of a specific European identity in relation to the superpowers that the West Europeans do not always possess. But what echo can this longing for a common ground with Western Europe in the search for independence and progress find; and how much can it retain, held in the straitjacket of determining military and economic factors?

It was only during one period, recently, that the straitjacket seemed to loosen slightly and the echo seemed to be there. Between the death of Stalin and the invasion of Prague or, more specifically, between 1953 and 1968, the East European freedom of maneuver and the interest thereby aroused in the West were on the increase. For the first time, it seemed that the continent's fate would be influenced as much, if not more, by the dialogue between the two Europes than by that of the two superpowers. It is interesting to recall the reasons for this phenomenon and the characteristics of that period, in order to understand the hopes it gave rise to and the disillusionment of the present period.

From Détente Based on Change . . .

The first sign came from the East, in the form of differentiation in the communist world and détente with the West. Both these tendencies; though partial, limited, subject to halts and regressions when they went too far, have survived these difficulties, especially the first. Malenkov's new course and Khrushchev's attempt to give a more dynamic and flexible character to both the party's leading role and that of the Soviet Union did, of course, lead to the uprisings in Berlin and Budapest. But Poland retained something of its October for a long time, Hungary began to develop again a few years after its own October, while the spirit of Camp David held sway less than two years after the Berlin Wall and six months after the Cuban crisis. More than anything else, the conflict with China and Albania, as well as the Rumanian heresy, seemed to herald what some commentators were already referring to as the breakdown of the Soviet empire in Eastern Europe.

In the West, after the happy conclusion of the Cuban crisis and the end of the Berlin crisis, the feeling of a Soviet threat ceased to provide fuel for the Cold War. The only real remaining obstacle to détente and, at the same time, to the division of Europe seemed to be the German problem. The division of Germany, both a reason for and consequence of the Cold War, has since the war been the only real link between the two Europes, embodied in concrete form by the status of Berlin, by intra-German trade (considered by the Common Market as internal trade), and so on.

From the moment that each of the two Europes began to be differentiated by limited polycentrism in the East and the adoption of more national policies in the West, particularly by France, the fate of the two Germanies became a more vital problem. Germany would not be reunited by military pressure. The West's attitude—no détente without reunification—became increasingly untenable because all the West Europeans, apart from Germany, had more interest in détente for themselves than reunification for their neighbor, and because German public opinion no longer believed that all they had to do was wait for a peace treaty to give them reunification. Whence the idea that it could only be approached by way of a detour, provided by European détente. Instead of making reunification a precondition for détente, or making solution of the German problem a precondition for solving the European problem, the idea of a parallel approach and then of an actual reversal of priorities was increasingly gaining ground.

From then on, the doors were open for all sorts of contacts, indirect maneuvers, and combinations. The question was no longer whether one should engage in negotiations, but rather of knowing who would conduct or control them and who would talk to whom: West Germany, France, West Europe, NATO, the United Sates? With the G.D.R., the other states of Eastern Europe, the Soviet Union? Different plans combined or stood in opposition to each other: "little steps" and "Wandel durch Annäherung" in Germany, "Europe from the Atlantic to the Urals" in France, "peaceful engagement" or "bridge-building" in the United States.

To begin with, in Germany, the emphasis was placed on maintaining if only minimal links between the two Germanies to keep open the chances for a future reunification, as well as on efforts to humanize relations within the nation. As attempts at negotiating with Moscow and attempts at making contact with Pankow seemed to offer no prospects, Bonn turned to the countries of Eastern Europe, in particular those, like Rumania, who were prepared to engage upon a dialogue, not only of an economic nature, like the others, but also diplomatic. The hope was that good relations with all the communist countries would in the end soften the inflexible attitude of those countries whose cooperation was vital—namely, the Soviet Union and the German Democratic Republic.

The second attempt was de Gaulle's. It was in his vision that the rebirth of national policies in Eastern Europe, which he had predicted since 1945, was given the most decisive role. His premise was that, henceforth, the national considerations would be more important than ideological ones, and this would apply to the Soviet Union just as much as to the satellites. He estimated that on account of the latter's resistance and primarily on account of the Chinese threat, the Soviet Union would feel prepared to withdraw somewhat from Eastern Europe: to adopt a style of domination more tolerant to national independence and outside influences (such as that of France) in exchange for greater influence and security in the West, to be brought about by an American withdrawal and a new status for Germany. In its turn, Germany would accept its frontiers and limitations on its armaments in exchange for some softening of its division. Soviet interests would then coincide with those of France, wanting above all to free itself—and Western Europe at the same time—from American hegemony, all the while continuing to contain Germany to a certain extent. De Gaulle envisioned the substitution of a broader and more flexible form of containment, based on an agreement of states, for the former, more rigid manner of containment, based on the respective integration of the two Europes. For this, France would have to position itself as intermediary between Germany and the Soviet Union and, with this end in view, use its influence with the states of Eastern Europe, full of distrust as they are of their two powerful neighbors, encouraging them to work their way, at the same time, into the new dialogue.

Indeed, for Americans such as Brzezinski, adviser to President Johnson in 1966-1967, and Henry Kissinger, it was important to take German and European aspirations to reunification into account while integrating them into a more global perspective, which would give a more positive significance to Atlantic ties and to the dialogue between the two great powers. A direct dialogue between Bonn and Moscow or Bonn and Pankow would be dangerous; on the other hand, de Gaulle and Europe generally did not have the means to match their vision. The general direction taken by Europe was right, but it could not meet with success in Moscow without American support. For Kissinger, the emphasis was on negotiations relating to the political-military future of Germany. To Brzezinski, it seemed the emphasis should be placed on a convergence of economic interests: a new Marshall Plan designed for Eastern Europe should be put forward; the special-ized institutions of the West, such as OECD, should be opened to Eastern Europe, which should eventually, bring the Soviet Union into a network of interdependence and of functional and multilateral ties that would make the ideological opposition and even the very existence of the East German satellite appear an anachronism, marked for progressive disappearance.

. . . To détente Within the Status Quo

The nature of these different plans and the rivalries they gave rise to, give us an idea of the varying dilemmas that confront all policies towards Eastern Europe and which, ever since 1967, have seemed doomed to paralyze any such initiatives. These dilemmas are posed below.

(1) Should East Germany be treated Like Other States? From the West German minister Schröder, through de Gaulle, to Brzezinski and Kissinger—all have drawn a distinction between the other communist states, which correspond more or less to some national reality, and the German Democratic Republic, an artificial creation that would become isolated in the process of détente and that a European settlement, accompanied by a withdrawal of occupying forces, would condemn to extinction. Nevertheless, though the states of Eastern Europe, particularly those who had no immediate fear of a reunited Germany, were ready enough to dissociate their policies from those of East Germany, the latter country and the Soviet Union were keeping a careful watch and in 1967 managed to impose a policy of solidarity on the whole bloc, except for Rumania. On the other hand, German public opinion, in particular the inhabitants of Berlin, did not take kindly to initiatives intended to isolate and exclude the G.D.R. from the benefits of détente; the seventeen million East German compatriots, after all, were the very people

with whom they wanted to maintain or reestablish links. From 1967, the policy of isolating East Germany was finished; this, however, meant that the frontier of the two Germanys became as intangible as the German-Polish frontier and that, for the foreseeable future, détente in Germany would assume the form desired by the Soviet Union—namely, through the maintenance of the status quo. The state of division would be certainly confirmed and possibly consolidated—albeit somewhat humanized in the most favorable case.

(2) Should the states of Eastern Europe or the Soviet Union be approached first? It is evident that any response of an exclusive nature would be disastrous. To go straight to the Kremlin would amount to helping consolidate its empire, with the effect of making it yet more rigid and exclusive. On the other hand, to try and encourage division in this empire and detach the weakest links would amount not only to alienating the Soviet Union, but would produce counterreactions on her part that would only render heavier the very yoke one had intended to lighten. Even if one approached the different communist countries in all innocence, letting them decide for themselves what Big Brother would tolerate and what risks they themselves might take, this too might yield the same result. In order to circumnavigate these reefs, one must first suppose either—as de Gaulle—that the Soviet Union is prepared to withdraw because of their preoccupation with China if given guarantees, or—as Brzezinski—that the Soviet Union is so attracted by the promises of Western technology that it would let itself be drawn into some common system that would dilute its authority. Secondly, this presupposes that the dynamic influence of an opening to the West and of internal liberalization would not escape the control of the communist leaders of the different countries, and that it would not involve them in an abrupt rupture with the Soviet system. There is too great a chasm between the conservative, police-minded Soviet Union and the exasperated population of Eastern Europe; the margin of action both of the local leaders and external powers is too narrow not to make brutal ups and downs much more likely than harmonious syntheses.

Thus, Western Germany has moved from a perhaps imprudent preference for the states of Eastern Europe in spite of Moscow's opposition, as was the case under Schröder, to what might be termed a slightly inelegant preference for Moscow ever since the invasion of Prague.

Under de Gaulle, France seemed to possess a clearer grasp of the situation and engaged in a more methodical attempt at balancing between the Soviet Union and its allies; yet this policy too was not lacking in ambiguity and contradictions. "Europe from the Atlantic to the Urals" on occasion seemed to signify a Franco-Soviet agreement that would replace Soviet-American hegemony; on other occasions, it signified a revolt of European nations, both East and West, against both hegemonies. De Gaulle visited the Soviet Union before Eastern Europe, and then Poland—the Soviet Union's orthodox ally—before he visited Rumania—"the Gaullist of the East." Nonetheless, in 1967 and 1968, during these journeys, he made speeches everywhere that went far beyond the accepted formulae, calling for national independence or the emergence of an autonomous Central Europe. On the other hand, he seems to have done nothing on a diplomatic level to lend support to Rumania and Yugoslavia, either in their day to day concerns, or after Prague when they feared a Soviet invasion; nor did he make the slightest gesture of a public nature to try and stop the invasion or to limit repression in Czechoslovakia. Quite the opposite, France was the first Western country to help the Soviet Union recreate a legitimate image for itself, the first after the Prague invasion to pretend that nothing essential had changed, while its own policy in relation to the East, was moving more and more towards an acceptance of the concept of division and détente based on the status quo.

Finally, on the American side, the evolution and the fluctuations were even more pronounced. Peaceful engagement in Eastern Europe had, in the beginning, been seen by such theoreticians as Brzezinski as an attempt to detach the satellites. Then the United States moved to a more multilateral concept, which included the Soviet Union, but kept the German Democratic Republic in isolation. Finally, a version has been adopted that includes everybody and is based, in fact, on accepting the status quo in the hope that—by giving it a multilateral and cooperative character—their most recalcitrant opposite numbers, the Soviet Union and the German Democratic Republic, would emerge from it transformed.

In reality, increasing emphasis was placed on bilateral détente with the Soviet Union: the American indifference towards the Soviet invasion in 1968 and the Moscow Agreement, followed by a visit to Poland in 1972, are the two clearest symbols of this development. Yet the same Johnson in the autumn of 1968, was uttering energetic, if ambiguous, warnings against any attempt to invade Rumania and Yugoslavia; and the same Nixon visited Rumania and Yugoslavia in 1969 and 1970 before going to Moscow and Warsaw, to the great displeasure of the Soviet Union. Thus one cannot be sure of the behavior of the United States in a violent crisis, particularly if it were to take place in Yugoslavia, nor underestimate the Nixon administration's predilection for showing the Soviet Union that it can cause troubles for the latter with its allies, a tendency also apparent in its China policy.

All in all one can say that the present trend is distinctly one of agreement with the Soviet Union, founded on an acceptance of the latter's authority in its own sphere, and that any concern to encourage an evolution in the nature of this authority does not, to put it mildly, seem to hold a very prominent place in the preoccupations of America's planetary diplomacy.

(3) Destalinization or desatellization? The third and fourth dilemmas are implicit in the first two. Basically they have to do with the question of whether preeminence should be given to societies or to states, both in the East and the West. The third dilemma has its source in the distinction, often made when observing the evolution of Eastern Europe, between destalinization or *internal liberalization* and desatellization or *external liberation.* It seems that in the long run both tendencies may well converge: the case of Yugoslavia shows that it broke with the Soviet Union purely to save its national independence, but the conflict with the Soviet Union forced it to seek for a new legitimacy of its own and to open up to the West. When the Soviet threat had declined, these two tendencies then led it to

grant increasing freedom both to intellectuals and to the different national groupings. Moreover, at the moment, one is witnessing in Yugoslavia a hardening in internal matters and a rapprochement with the Soviet Union in external affairs—a negative sign indicating that the two tendencies are indeed related. Nevertheless, in the case of Albania (not to mention China), total desatellization has not led to any liberalization, quite the contrary; or the case of Hungary buying its internal reforms at the price of total orthodoxy in external affairs; or Rumania, where the primary concern for external independence has considerably reduced arbitrariness from above when compared with the period before 1964, but has not led to any initiative from below; or the case of Poland, where Gierek, who is more responsive to the needs of the population than Gomulka, has been, so far seeking far less than the latter did to play any real role in external affairs.

Now one is confronted by the three-fold problem: what do the countries of Eastern Europe want most? What is the Soviet Union most likely to tolerate? What developments do the Western countries have the most compelling interest in encouraging?

The Prague Spring was directed at internal change, not opposition to the Soviet Union. Yet, inasmuch as the Soviet Union felt its own authority to be threatened by this internal transformation, the question of external independence as a condition of internal reform and the question of resisting pressure or indeed the invasion were inevitably raised—no matter what the Czechoslovaks themselves might have preferred. If one is then led to conclude in favor of the Rumanian way (seek political independence first, and the rest will come later), one is tempted to think (along with the Rumanian population) that without internal reform, especially in the economic sphere, one runs the risk of not possessing the means for any kind of external independence other than verbal and that if the leaders—whether to reassure the Soviet Union or to protect the country from the latter's possible actions—continue to reinforce centralization, this is a heavy price to pay for a spectacular and acrobatic foreign policy. The example of Czechoslovakia shows the merit of the

Rumanian model; a certain stagnation of the latter lends value to the Hungarian way.

Faced with the extremely limited freedom of maneuver of these countries, given the impossibility of foreseeing the criteria and limits of Soviet tolerance (each intervention having invalidated the rules seemingly implied by previous experience), and faced by the fact that it is impossible for these populations to express their preferences—those of the Western nations are hardly likely to be decisive. Yet, to a certain extent they, either indirectly or explicitly, have to make a choice.

Thus West Germany, concerned above all with the fate of the German Democratic Republic, sees that the latter depends above all on its ties with Moscow. In the final analysis, only independence from Moscow would make it possible to change the East German regime; yet in reality, since this radical change will most likely never take place, it is, paradoxically, West Germany that must rely on greater influence from Moscow to soften the position of the GDR. In any case, if the aim is no longer to achieve national reunification, it is much more to improve the fate of the population in the German Democratic Republic than to increase the freedom of action of its government.

Similarly, the American position, inasmuch as it no longer aims to detach the satellite countries from the Soviet Union, can only point to the benefits of general détente for the internal development of these societies. Contrary to this, French policies under de Gaulle were favorable, on principle, to the independence of these states, but disdainful of ideology and internal regimes —hence, the lack of interest and support for the Czechoslovak experience, judged to be the work of intellectuals who were incompetent on the diplomatic level.

4. What development do we hope for? From this example, one can see clearly that the preferences shown for Eastern Europe, spring in the first place from those one has for oneself. This brings us to the fourth dilemma, which includes all the others, because it raises the question of what concept we have of international life and of politics itself: on what grounds should we struggle, and what should we encourage? Does one think in

terms of *states, political regimes,* or *social structures?* Apart from
the choices that we cannot make for others and the direct
influence we are unable to exercise over them, what choices are
we making for ourselves and what indirect influence will they
have on the development of these other nations?

To the extent that what happens to Western Europe may have
value as an example or a magnet for Eastern Europe, one can see
a basic opposition between giving priority to the independence of
states and emphasising the interdependence of societies. According to the first, the more we retain our sovereignty, the more
we detach ourselves from the United States, the more we
encourage the countries of Eastern Europe to live up to their
national personalities and detach themselves from the Soviet
Union. According to the second concept, the more successful we
are in creating a zone of cooperation and prosperity, forgetting
old quarrels, the more the countries of Eastern Europe will tend
to feel reassured by this stability, attracted by this prosperity,
drawn into this cooperation. On one side, priority is placed on
the breaking up of the present blocs, without any clear idea of
what would succeed them; on the other, priority is placed on sub-
and supranational links, stretching increasingly between West and
East, depriving conflicts and sovereignty of any real meaning. In
both cases, there would be a decline in the role of ideology, to
the benefit either of a differentiation of national interests, or of
the convergence of modern societies.

Gone with the tanks! They were the messengers of the
counterrevolutionary Holy Alliance, just as the barricades of Paris
had heralded the contagious nature of revolts. The two had this
much in common: they shattered the illusion of the death of
ideology, an illusion shared in common by the nostalgics of the
European concert and the prophets of the technetronic age. For a
Europe based on the irresistible pull, either of national will or of
technological convergence, to have a chance at all, the Soviet
Union, which possesses the military power, would have had to
subscribe to the concept of its interests that resembled that of its
Western partners more than its present Caesaropapist one.
Reminding everyone that it has the last word (that is, the big
battalions), the Soviet Union made it clear that, contrary to de

Gaulle's hopes, conflict with China would serve to encourage it in strengthening its authority in its empire rather than withdrawing from it, and that, contrary to the hopes of Brzezinski, it was in fact the Soviet Union that held its satellites back and not they that carried the Soviet Union toward the West.

The trend towards rapprochement does exist, but is always blocked because the country that is least close to the West happens to be the most powerful. Thus, when the process of European convergence really gets going, the countries of Central Europe like Czechoslovakia immediately find themselves too far ahead on the way to a common civilization and language with Western Europe for it not to cause anxiety to the Soviet leaders and for them not to put the brakes on. To the Soviets, developments are only acceptable if they can be controlled. So they never go far enough, for fear of going too far: the Soviet Union has no desire to sacrifice the two birds in the hand for one bird in the bush—i.e., for a European reconciliation, economic and technical cooperation, and an extension of her influence in the West, all of which to her seem fraught with risks and less vital than her rule in Eastern Europe.

This reaction, which could have been foreseen for a long time, became increasingly evident after 1967. What is most astonishing is that, having chosen the priority of consolidation in Eastern Europe with the most brutal clarity, the Soviet Union nowadays seems to be winning—so to speak, as a bonus—in the other sphere too. She seems on the way to obtaining the European reconciliation, the economic and technical cooperation, the growing influence in the West—promised by Western strategies before 1968—without having to make the concessions and furnish the guarantees that the latter initially demanded. She can eat her East European cake and have her Western détente too.

Traditionally, the Soviet Union had to face a double dilemma: on the one hand, rigidity in the East or détente in the West; on the other hand, cooperation with the United States to maintain the status quo or with the West Europeans to diminish American influence. Today, with the confirmation of Soviet power in Eastern Europe, with Western acceptance of this fait accompli, with the American trend toward withdrawal and the uncertainties of Europe—all these factors seem to combine, giving all these trends simultaneous sway. A conservative hardening has taken place inside and active détente outside; while cooperation with the United States is combined with a certain progress at the latter's expense, shaping the situation in a way beneficial to the Soviet Union.

Traditionally, periods of détente, favorable as they are to pluralism, presented more problems to the Soviet Union than to the West. This time, however, the combination of Western crises and the Soviet success in applying a miraculous cure to the ills of polycentrism (one that could hardly be used in Western Europe: armed intervention) seems to have led to a détente, which, at least in the short term, is more favorable to the Soviet Union than to its allies and its rivals.

Normalization and the Normal

Here again, most surprising is not that détente survived the intervention in Czechoslovakia, but that so soon after, on both sides, things went so much farther than before 1968. The Soviet Union put forward the idea of a conference on European Security in 1954 and then again in 1965; it was, however, after its third launching in the spring of 1969 that the idea was first accorded a favorable reception, and that it now will almost certainly take place. Germany put out feelers under Adenauer, then engaged in a more or less full-scale Eastern policy under Schröder and the Kiesinger-Brandt great coalition; yet it was after 1968 (even before Willy Brandt came to power—in fact, in the spring of 1969) that the Soviet Union played the card it had always held in reserve till then: to include Germany in the process of détente and, in so doing, to give up its role as unifying scarecrow of the bloc.

It is evident that the main explanation lies in the success of the intervention in Czechoslovakia, similar to the other avowal of failure in the East which also proved a source of success in relations with the West: the Berlin Wall. In both cases, the move reassured the Soviet and East German leaders that they could control the process of détente by stopping it abruptly, if it should get out of hand. Since then, they have had less need of an external threat as a unifying factor; force is enough, especially as it crushes any hopes for reunification held by the peoples of Eastern Europe and by the Western powers, in particular Germany. Now that there is no longer any hope of changing the status quo or of affecting the evolution, the hour of normalization has struck.

Another evolution of Soviet attitudes also seems to go in the direction of a greater acceptance of the status quo: Moscow has considerably diminished the anti-American aspect of its policy on European security; it hardly disguises any longer its acceptance of existing alliances. On the other hand, the Soviet government hopes that détente in the form of treaties with Federal Germany and the security conference, will square the circle by consolidating its sphere of domination in Eastern Europe, by confirming its legitimacy, by showing both recalcitrant peoples and governments that there is no point in harboring any more illusions about Western support.

In this respect, the recognition, particularly by Germany, that it is necessary to come to terms with the Soviet Union before Poland and Czechoslovakia and to count on its influencing the German Democratic Republic in the right way, is particularly important. In the same way, the European Security Conference is a perfect symbol both of détente and of the acceptance of the status quo, understood as meaning the consequences not only of the Second World War but also of the second Prague coup.

For all this, what uncertainties attend this calculation; how riddled with worms the fruit of this status quo; what ambiguity and contradiction surrounds the horrible term "normalization"! Procrustus, expert as he was in normalizing his friends and guests, could well be counted if not as its inventor, at least as its hero. The word "normalization" is used every day for relations between the West, in particular Germany, and the communist world, and for the process of getting Czechoslovakia back into line. That the pacified and reconciled Europe of détente, entente, and cooperation should at the same time be the one where, four years after the invasion, Soviet troops are still in Czechoslovakia, where men are sentenced by the courts for having advocated that people boycott the elections, while in the Soviet Union itself, dissenters are "normalized" in psychiatric clinics—all this may be understood as a form of realism. Yet, it cannot help bringing to mind the cry of a Czechoslovak writer, "We live in a world where madmen put straightjackets on sane people."

What relation is there between these two forms of normalization: that of East-West relations and that of the Soviet empire? One is probably the essential precondition of the other: only the normalization of Czechoslovakia—that is, absolute control over the empire—gives the Soviet Union enough confidence to begin normalizing this empire's relations with the outside world. But what impact does the second form of normalization have on the first?

This for us is the heart of the matter, and it is at this point that we enter into the realm of supposition and contradictory guesses. Does external normalization have any effect on internal normalization, does it render the latter all the more irrevocable by legitimizing it; or, on the other hand, does it point up the abnormality of it by removing the alibi of security? Indeed, in the long run, will external normalization transform the internal situation in its own image—into a normality that is peaceful, tolerant and flexible?

Obviously the West, and particularly the Brandt government, places its bets on the last hypothesis. The Soviet Union, however, can only make the opposite gamble, whether it believes in the opposite effect, or whether it is prepared to accept risks (which it believes will be limited and controllable) in Eastern Europe for the sake of an active policy towards the West.

Hence the quetions: *What, in the present phase, is considered "normal" in Western Europe?* Would it consist of a return to its actual geographical situation as the Western point of a Eurasian land mass where the Soviet Union would command the dominant position dictated by its size? Is it rather a Europe of détente, where the Common Market and even the American presence would be considered normal, but where the creation of a political and military Europe would constitute a dangerous development, whose abnormal nature would be shown up precisely by the normalization of East-West relations? From now on, all speculations on the second thoughts and strategies of both sides are permitted for the simple reason that—with the official recognition of the status quo, with the official acceptance of détente, and the increase in contacts between the two halves of Europe—we have entered, no doubt for a long time, into the era of ambiguity, uncertainty, and gambles.

This is exactly what, in our minds, appears to distinguish the present international reality most from its historical precedents; and, for example, what distinguishes the military intervention in Czechoslovakia from other occupations, the German-Soviet treaty from other negotiations, the European Security Conference from other conferences. Rarely have force and diplomacy rested on such implicit gambles about their effects on long-term historical, political, and economic, but above all psychological or social processes. Yet nobody knows to what extent they can be manipulated, reversed, influenced, controlled, or limited by troops and treaties.

In the long run, who can possibly pretend to know whether the invasion will secure or compromise Soviet influence in Eastern Europe, whether the meaning of Ostpolitik lies in the acceptance of German division or in the adoption of the one possible way to surmount it, if the Eastern Security Conference will favor the unity of the blocs or their dissolution? In other ages, force and diplomacy permitted conquests and the reversal of alliances. During the Cold War, such modifications of the status quo were impossible. The situation was frozen in confrontation, the two blocs welded by the threat, real or supposed, of the enemy—with the status quo upheld by the fact that nobody recognized it.

There is thus a two-fold paradox in this current era of negotiation. On the one hand, all this spectacular activity amounts basically to recognizing the status quo. Yet, on the other hand, this recognition of the status quo could activate psychological and social forces that would undermine it far more powerfully, because more unpredictably, than all diplomatic or military undertakings now being contemplated.

The Uncertainties of Détente

What characterizes the situation in Europe is above all the contrast between the rigidity of the system on a state and international level, and the fragility of societies—the continuation of structures that have lost their deep legitimacy yet have retained enough power to show up the weakness of those who challenge them. Among blocs, alliances, or regional organizations, rivalry no longer leads to conquest or even to active subversion. It becomes a matter of "competitive decadence," of comparative resistance to the forces of disintegration which eat away at all of them and which will be encouraged by their mutual acceptance and interpenetration. The Cold War was in fact characterized by the triumph of the defensive, hidden and protected by verbal offensive. Policies of normalization or détente do not necessarily disturb the balance between alliances or societies, but they do tend to make them much more vulnerable to each other. From the moment the existence or legitimacy of social structures is recognized, real competition, whether intentional or not, begins: it relates to their content, their comparative degree of dynamism, and their unity.

Within any particular institutional framework, there is room for considerable variation in the balance of wills, of hopes, and influences. A sort of "hot peace" is increasingly replacing the Cold War. In relation to the latter, this new peace has the same relation as the Cold War had to war: it is a step further away from the use of force and aggression against the opposite system. Yet the threats against the solidarity of the systems themselves have not necessarily diminished.

In this new phase of ambiguity and contradiction, isolation can be broken, but only in favor of an asymmetric and unbalanced penetration rather than of reconciliation. There may always be enough communication and convergence to prevent stabilization by isolation, enough separation and divergence to prevent stabilization by integration. The main characteristic of the "hot peace" is neither force nor cooperation, but the constant reciprocal influence of societies within the framework of a competition whose goals are less and less tangible, whose means are less and less direct, whose consequences are less and less calculable—precisely because they have to do with activities rather than strategies, and indeed because these activities are important by their effect on what societies *are* as much as on what they do.

Power considerations retain their importance, but within this complex process (where the Soviet Union is increasingly superior militarily, and the Western countries are superior on the economic and technical level), the most decisive element is in fact the crisis, both social and spiritual, of modern society. This crisis is more visible and diffuse in the West, it is more controlled but more explosive in the East. The brutality of communist regimes makes them better at repressing dissidents while the elasticity of Western societies makes them better at coopting them. At the present, Soviet imperial authority, both inside and outside the bloc, is expanding, yet always exposed to explosions; in the West, the main threat is rather erosion.

If this is so, the same process of détente can encourage the external successes of the Soviet Union and aggravate its internal difficulties by setting the cycle of liberalization, explosion, repression. In the West, détente can help the economy by reducing military expenses, but also contribute to ideological disintegration and a waning of authority in external affairs, passing from moralistic pacifism to resigned or unavowed dependence. At which point Europe would as a rule have to adopt the most reassuring interpretation possible of Soviet policy precisely because it needed reassurance. The word "Finland-ization" has often been used in this context. If it means the difference between the internal regime and the external situation, the ambiguity of an influence usually exercized over external policies and only exceptionally over internal ones, one could then say that both Western and Eastern Europe can at the same time either fear or hope for such a process of Finlandization. One would have less freedom of external action and the other would have more freedom for internal development.

The problem of the present period is: *who will Finlandize whom?* Will the process of détente have the effect of making things difficult for a coherent Western Europe capable of action, by drowning it in a pan-European group dominated by the Soviet Union? Or will it rather transform the latter's empire into a classical sphere of influence? Will it give rise to a slow erosion of ideological barriers or to abrupt explosions with unforeseeable consequences? The anxiety of the Soviet leaders in confronting the revolt in Gdansk in December 1970 clearly indicates that this hypothesis cannot be excluded, that in fact it is in the very nature of a system that allows no peaceful expression of opposition. If, however, Eastern Europe is in a state of permanent instability, it is still the situation of the Soviet Union that is decisive, and the latter seems to be far less fragile.

In the West, northern Europe, which is relatively stable politically, is increasingly exposed to the psychological effects of Soviet military might. In the south, the instability of societies and regimes, from the Balkans to the Spanish peninsula, raises the spectre of internal conflict and external interventions.

The vital spots are Yugoslavia and the two Germanys. Yugoslavia is threatened both by erosion and explosion, by social and nationl conflicts, subject to the influence of capitalist society and to the watchful and not always reassuring concern of the Soviet Union—always ready to profit from the divisions in Yugoslav society to reaffirm its socialist solidarity.

As for central Europe, it is a zone of balance unlike the north, and of stability unlike the south. It is also the region where the two countries most representative of the two systems are in most contact and in the most decisive manner. If West Germany were too weak or too strong, if it were either "Finlandized" or aggressive, if East Germany were attracted by it, or were the victim of any violent agitation—it would in one way or another call into question the whole balance of the continent. Indeed the swiftness of mental transformation in Germany leads us to think that after having been the most predictable country of Europe, Germany is now again beginning to display the famous and worrying "incertitudes allemandes."

The policies of the Soviet Union seem to display a very lucid awareness of this new state of fluidity with its dangers and possibilities. Not a day passes in the Soviet Union and all the countries of Eastern Europe but there is a call for ideological vigilance, which runs the risk of being lulled by the process of détente, or an exhortation to continue the anti-imperalist struggle, at the same time taking a stand against the Cold War and for the dissolution of the blocs. Not a day without protests against "psychological warfare" or ideological contraband from the West, while ideological struggle is waged against the convergence of societies. The communist countries' restrictive attitude to the theme of the "free movement of people and ideas" shows how defensive they feel in this respect. They are trying to acquire the economic and technical benefits of détente, while avoiding intellectual and social contagion by keeping up ideological hostility and by a certain physical isolation.

On the other hand, their Soviet attitude toward the comparative evolution of the two systems is optimistic. In a report on Western Europe in the 1970s, prepared by the top Soviet specialists for the Central Committee, the points emphasized were the American trend toward withdrawal, the aggravation of conflict between capitalist countries, the cultural and moral crisis of Western society (which, it is supposed, will assume particularly serious dimensions in Germany), and, by contrast, the necessity of reinforcing the integration, unity, and dynamism of the socialist camp (see Tatu, 1972: 7). The expectation and exploitation of "social disintegration" takes precedence over the more classic expectation of economic crisis. The outlook is neither one of war nor one of revolution, but that of a patiently expected and discretely encouraged evolution.

That is how we must interpret the Soviet Union's perception of Western realities. It does not seek to blockade Berlin, nor to engineer the neutralization of Germany, the dissolution of the Common Market, or the departure of American troops from Europe. Nevertheless, within the existing legal and social structures, it desires a Berlin as detached as possible from the Federal Republic, a Federal Republic as detached as possible from Western Europe, Western societies as divided as possible—as long as these circumstances do not lead to upheavals that might call Soviet authority in its own zone into question. It recognizes Western realities, but in order to change them.

In an even more prudent, though perhaps less lucid and systematic way, this is also the approach of the German Ostpolitik. In this sense, one can contrast the policies of Brezhnev and Brandt with those of Khrushchev and de Gaulle. The latter attacked the European order frontally, whether it concerned

Berlin or the existence of alliances or blocs. Brezhnev and Brandt have both understood that the only chance of modifying the status quo was to start by accepting it. This was already true of the German Ostpolitik sketched out before 1968. But at that time it was a question of accepting a part of the status quo (basically, the territorial one) in order to modify another component (basically, the political one); the emphasis was more on changing than accepting. Now, on the other hand, the emphasis is reversed. The Federal Republic recognizes not only its frontiers but, in fact, the German Democratic regime and Soviet supremacy in Eastern Europe.

Like the Soviet Union, however, West Germany hopes that the processes of détente and communication will work in a way favorable to the former aims, now redefined in a more realistic —that is in a more modest and especially less immediate—way. The slight difference between Soviet and German policies is that the former do not content themselves with hoping. While all the time trying not to assume a worrying aspect, the Soviets exert a discreet but firm and constant pressure in favor of their objectives.

The efforts of Willy Brandt's Germany are, for the time being, directed more at proving its good will than at negotiation proper. Its main aim, at the present time, seems to be the creation of an atmosphere of confidence and cooperation, to which it attaches an intrinsic value and which, on the other hand, it hopes will encourage a favorable evolution. It is aware that this evolution is not certain; but the West German government believes that all attempts to exercise direct pressure in favor of the independence of states or the freedom of individuals in Eastern Europe would only arouse suspicion and irritation among the Soviet and East German leaders and would drive them to put a stop to the process. The whole point of Ostpolitik consists of showing them that nobody wants to sabotage their authority, or even help them to stabilize it, in the hope that once assured of its solidity, they will be able and willing to make it more flexible.

Prospects

Although the result is vague as regards both formulation and prospects, at least Germany has a coherent attitude (if not a policy) and a coherent perspective (if not a strategy). Can any other approach be adopted in this day and age?

Michel Tatu's excellent book (1972) on the subject calls on the West to assume a posture that is closer in spirit to that of the Soviet Union—i.e., tougher or more combative in short-term negotiations and placing less stress on vague concepts, such as "climate" or "détente," or on risky gambles:

> The one certain fact is that the Soviet leaders do not allow themselves to be impressed by a "climate," an eminently changeable thing and one that they can, moreover, modify at will. What counts for them is what can be got straightaway, on the spot; two birds in the bush are a small price for them to pay in return for one bird in the hand from the opposite camp.

Negotiations with the Soviet Union are excellent where give-and-take bargaining is involved; but it is dangerous for us to go about it with our hands tied, by making an irreversible commitment to détente and refraining from maximizing our gains or criticizing the Soviet Union so as not to allow the climate to worsen or for fear of "reverting to the Cold War." An approach of this kind would pave the way for Finlandization.

Tatu also accuses Western foreign policymakers of being too interested in the Soviet Union and insufficiently interested in Eastern Europe. The Soviet Union is bound to dominate in any dialogue, at least until a European federation can form a power capable of redressing the balance. In the absence of such a federation, the only acceptable European equilibrium would be based on the countries of Western Europe being balanced out by the small and medium-sized states of Eastern Europe. The East European states should be the preferred negotiating partners for Western Europe, closer as they are in culture and feeling and less dangerous because of their smaller size.

Tatu (1972: 48) is obviously aware of the eternal dilemma (in relation to Western Europe, as noted earlier, Eastern Europe is too strong if the Soviet Union is included, and too weak if she is excluded), and of the crushing argument that the Soviet Union has the means of preventing this kind of dialogue between

Eastern and Western Europe. He too takes refuge in long-term hopes:

> This is no reason for agreeing, in the name of a somewhat short-sighted "realism," to adhere to the views of the Kremlin and agree to schemes which run the risk of being proved embarrassingly wrong ten years later. The success of a policy cannot be judged by the length of time which it takes to reach solutions, but by the quality of the solutions and the length of time they will endure. In the meantime it would be better to do nothing rather than act in the opposite direction from the "optimum" solution.

This must certainly be the only really worthwhile and serious debate about our approach to Eastern Europe. Like all valid debates, it has no obvious winner. It involves a post-Prague version of the second and third dilemmas we have outlined earlier. It corresponds, seen from Eastern Europe, to the distinction between the Rumanian and the Hungarian roads (which have been dubbed, respectively, the "intra-bloc nationalist" and the "consumer" deviations). These can be broken down into the argument as to whether the Soviet Union should be challenged for the sake of independence on the part of small and medium-sized states, or whether society should be reformed and the lot of the population improved while avoiding at all costs conflict with the Soviet Union in foreign policy. Tatu is obviously an admirer of the Rumanian method, whereas Willy Brandt bases his policies on the same hypotheses as the Hungarian approach. In both cases, moreover, it is how the communist world itself evolves that appears to be the decisive factor, rather than Western policies whose real importance is normally only marginal, although it can doubtless be important in Soviet decision-making at times of crisis.

Perhaps Tatu underestimates the importance of the opening of the East, of gradually strengthening networks of communications and interdependence, while Brandt underestimates their potentially explosive effects. Perhaps Tatu gives too much credit to the Soviet leaders' capacity for avoiding the social, political, and ideological side-effects while Brandt puts too much hope in Soviet willingness to put up with them. Perhaps Tatu—especially writing after the Prague invasion—also overestimates the room for maneuver possessed by small and medium-sized European states, while Brandt has surely underestimated the resentment aroused in Eastern Europe by the fact that he chose to talk first to Moscow.

When all is said, it certainly seems that the only hope lies in the dimension chosen by the German Ostpolitik—that of a long-term process within the existing framework. But with regard to the way the countries of the West are playing their respective parts in this process, Tatu is certainly right to deplore their lack of dynamism, lack of confidence in their case, and lack of solidarity with the East Europeans. This criticism is valid when applied to three issues: reciprocity in short-term talks, a long-term all-European project, and abandonment of double-talk.

Viewed in the light of these three considerations, the German Ostpolitik is obviously somewhat flabby, but the policies of other Western countries are still more so. In his Nobel Prize speech, Brandt gave quite a penetrating analysis of the aims of his policies. He said that they were designed: (1) to strengthen German freedom of maneuver, but this went hand in hand with a renunciation of great power ambitions; (2) to maintain existing alliances and institutions, but expanded in scope and eventually modified in meaning by pan-European cooperation; and (3) to safeguard the balance of national interests, but within the framework of and on behalf of a "European and world internal policy" (*Weltinnenpolitik*) that would look after the interests of men and societies as much as of nations and states.

In France, by contrast, it would not be too unjust to say that government policies towards the East are a mixture of Atlantic orthodoxy and pro-Soviet leanings in the name of the dissolution of power blocs; while the attitude of the left is a brew made up of Wilsonian-type utopianism and acceptance of the Brezhnev doctrine in the name of socialism and democracy.

The French have begun to take seriously the prospect of an eventual American withdrawal and consequent Soviet military superiority. This has led them, in certain respects, to become the staunchest supporters of NATO orthodoxy. They not only oppose the idea of American troop withdrawals but were, until recently, hostile to mutual balanced force reductions—despite the fact that certain states, either nonaligned or heretical communist in character, seek in these measures a protection against great power intervention. At the same time, the French want to maintain relations with the Soviet Union that are at least as cordial as those maintained by other countries. To do this France has chosen to be converted, with belated enthusiasm, to the idea of the European Security Conference. The reason for her conversion is that she considers the conference as unlikely to have any significant outcome. But at the same time, so as to profit from the gesture, France is embarrassed by an agenda likely to raise matters that will displease the Soviets. This is true even where the matters raised touch on principles that France does try to advocate.

The non-communist left, at least in France, protests against talk of the dangers of a Prague-style intervention or of the application of the Brezhnev doctrine to a socialist Western country. It bases its optimisim on its trust in the permanence of blocs. When accused, then, of basing the prospects of democratic socialism coming out on top of its communist allies in a potential coalition government upon the permanence of the Yalta partition and of the American military presence, its leaders declare that they do want to replace this bipolar order by an independent Europe. But they give no indication of the way to get there. Their only positive policies are reminiscent of the old three-point formula (arbitration, collective security, and disarmament) that was already quite unrealistic at the time of the League of Nations, let alone in the nuclear age! The non-communist left also has a tendency to accept Soviet-inspired proposals on European security, without any effort to adapt them to specifically European interests or to the cause of human rights.

Rather than accepting this combination of verbal condemnation and practical acceptance of the blocs, it may be more desirable, here as elsewhere, not to hide realities. These facts, inescapable for the time being, include the Soviet presence, the inescapable need for a military balance in Europe—whether Atlantic or continental, and the unacceptable character—for now and for ever—of the political and human consequences of this presence and of this balance: oppression and division, the closing of borders to individuals and their opening to tanks. Instead of seeking to reassure everyone by resorting to universal untruths on blocs and security, it would be more honest and more effective to speak frankly to the Soviet Union. The Russians should be told that nobody tries to suppress the role of great powers, but that our objective is to limit their tendency to exploit this role for oppressive ends. Existing blocs should be changed into alliances. This would mean that freely chosen alliances, balanced and limited in scope to foreign policies and defense, should take the place of ideological police-state groupings. Another aspect of our stated aims should be to create within the alliances and between them and nonaligned states, the same security that already exists between the two alliances and that has turned Europe, unlike Asia or the Middle East, into the continent of "the war which has not taken place."

It might be useful to employ the fourfold slogan of the Prague Spring: Socialism, Liberty, Alliance, and Sovereignty. Western countries would make a solemn declaration that they have no intention of acting against either the socialist structure of the countries of Eastern Europe or their membership in the Warsaw Pact. They would, however, make a no-less-solemn declaration that the degree of warmth in their relations with East European countries depends on the degree of the latter's internal liberties and external sovereignty. This policy would not aim at imposing on these countries our own definition of these concepts; peaceful coexistence, as the Soviets justly desire, must be applied to all regimes. On the other hand, mutual understanding, cooperation, participation in joint bodies and common undertakings, the spirit of community, and dialogue regarding any solid peace pre-supposes a minimum of reciprocity, common attitudes, mutually accepted definitions and rules of conduct.

This position could be applied both to the immediate level of day-to-day negotiations, in forming new pan-European insti-tutions perhaps stemming from the security conference itself, and to the more utopian and long-term concept of a reconciled Europe.

In the first stage, the search for common definitions of such notions as cultural cooperation, subversion, and nonintervention should lead to real reciprocity in commercial exchanges and communications, in the understanding of the limits with which they must be hedged for security considerations, and of the guarantees needed to prevent their abuse. Where the asymmetrical nature of political regimes or alliances or where differences inherent in the temporary ordering of priorities would prevent reciprocity eventually growing into symmetry, compensation and compromise should be sought.

States should be able to agree, for example, on the optimum number of cultural and technological exchanges. If one group cares more about the first and the other cares more about the second, they ought to be able to weigh the advantages of military security or political control against losses of potential economic advantage. Such weighing up of activities that are different in nature is certainly artificial and exceptional, but numerous precedents for this procedure do exist. In the late fifties and early sixties, lengthy negotiations between the United States and Hungary led to Hungary being fully reinstated in the United Nations in return for an amnesty for political prisoners. Other amnesties in other Eastern European countries have accompanied East-West commercial deals. Similar measures were taken by the G.D.R. to ease Willy Brandt's electoral position, and the treaty between the two Germanies does contain an implicit bargain of *"menschliche Erleichterungen"* against *"staatliche Anerkennung"*.

In the second stage, this kind of dialogue is the chief justification for accepting the idea of creating pan-European institutions. A commission on crises and conflicts could discuss differences arising from political, economic, and military matters. An arms control committee could monitor the introduction of measures designed to limit the freedom of action of the superpowers. A political assembly that would be consultative and would function on the consensus principle, rather than on majority vote, could give each state a chance to express its views in an arena broader than the framework of their respective alliances, yet narrower than the forum of the United Nations. A European commission for human rights, based on a pan-Europeanization of the European Declaration of Human Rights and of the institutions, built within the framework of the Council of Europe (such as the European Human Rights Commission and Court), which are functioning today to protect them, would be set up to hear the grievances of individuals and associations as well as of states.

It should not be forgotten that such institutions would serve as an instrument through which the Soviet Union could try to put a brake on the growth of a West European political or military entity. But West Europeans capable of uniting for a common project should be in a position to accept the risks likely to stem from accepting the logic of mutual free access and interpenetration, which is the only possible alternative to monolithic blocs and spheres of oppression.

A Third Voice

But has such a common plan any chance of seeing the light of day? Here we reach the third aspect—the most distant and uncertain one and yet probably the key to the other two. All the practical compromises and the temporary recognition of all the unpleasant realities can have real meaning if they are underlain by a real European project. What could this project be? Perhaps the gradual emergence within their respective present alliances and systems of a Western Europe and Eastern Europe whose dialogue would engender a third voice rather than a third force or a third way? Perhaps the combination of preferential ties between these two Europes and their respective superpowers, and between countries having common traditions transcending military and ideological barriers, like the two Germanies or the Balkan countries? Perhaps a dialogue between a European way to liberalism and a European way to communism which might end by defining at last the premises of a real democratic socialism? Today one can only speculate.

At any rate, it is not for governments to propose today the political and, even less, the ideological shape most desirable for a future Europe. But what about the intellectuals? What about the parties of the left? Can the Western left really be taken seriously if it ignores or forgets the international lessons to be drawn from the division of Europe, or if its critique of the existing structures and its search for a new model neglect the critiques and the explorations of the Polish October and the Prague Spring? Can one break out of the "silence of Europe" without breaking out of the double-talk and ignorance about Eastern Europe, without abandoning the cowardice that consists of not supporting efforts towards independence on the part of Soviet satellites (because we want peace with the Soviet Union), or, conversely, (in order not to embarrass the same East European states), of ignoring the appeals of oppressed individuals?

Two voices from the East put us in our place. The first is that of a Czechoslovak historian (Kusin, 1968: 48) writing to one of his friends who left the country in 1968. He asks his correspondent what concepts are being worked out in this Europe (which the Prague Spring wished to become part of) that could stimulate the rebirth of the reform and reconciliation movement the day the balance of power permits it. One can imagine the embarrassment of the recipient of the letter.

The other voice is that of Solzhenitsyn (1972) in his Nobel Prize essay. He takes the Western world to task for being able to say, when faced with a muddy swamp, "Oh, what a pretty little pool! " or, on seeing someone in heavy chains, "Oh, what a charming necklace! " The spirit of Munich, as far as Solzhenitsyn is concerned, is not so much nonresistance as the acceptance of the supreme sin—the absence of communication, a refusal by artists, intellectuals, and scientists to take up the miraculous gift which they alone possess, that of being able to cross frontiers and barbed wire fences at a time

> when there are no longer internal affairs on our overpopulated earth, and when the salvation of mankind depends on each of us making his neighbor's affairs his own and on the peoples of the East having a vital interest in what is being thought in the West, on the peoples of the West having overriding concern over what happens in the East.

Neither the balance of power, nor the preoccupations of the peoples of the West, nor the priorities of governments, nor the demands of technology hold out much hope for Eastern Europe to escape from the empire of force. As Solzhenitsyn says, only one weapon against violence remains, and that is the refusal to lie. If we need a utopia, let those who—in both East and West—have no power whatever remain faithful at least to the proverb which the Russian writer uses to end his speech: "A word of truth weighs more than the whole world."

REFERENCES

BRZEZINSKI, Z. (1972) "The balance of power illusion." Foreign Policy 7 (Summer).

BULL, H. (1970) "Soviet-American relations and world order." Adelphi Paper 65 (February).

DUCHENE, F. (1972) "Europe's contribution to world peace," p. 43 in R. Mayne (ed.) Europe Tomorrow. London: Fontana.

ELLSWORTH, R. (1972) "Deterrence in Europe in the 1970s: Washington attitudes." Roundtable (April): 147.

GASTEIGER, K. (1971) "The fragile balance: looking ahead at East-West relations." Interplay (March): 27-34.

HASSNER, P. (1972a) "L'Europe de l'Est, vue de loin." Esprit (December).

––– (1972b) "Between two ages or between two stools? (The implications of political change for European security and arms control)." Presented at the Conference on European Security, SALT, and U.S.-European Relations, Geneva, August 31-September 2.

––– (1968) "Change and security in Europe. I. The background." Adelphi Paper 45 (February).

HOFFMAN, S. (1972) "Weighing the balance of power." Foreign Affairs (July): 628-629.

HUGHES, T. (1972) "Whose century? " Foreign Affairs (July).

HUNT, K. (1973) "Some military alternatives for NATO," in European Security and the Nixon Doctrine: Report of a Conference. Medford, Mass.: Fletcher School of Law and Diplomacy (February).

KUSIN, V. (1968) The Intellectual Origins of the Prague Spring. London: Cambridge Univ. Press.

NEHRLICH, U. (1973) "Alternative strategic and tactical doctrines in the Central European theatre," in European Security and the Nixon Doctrine: Report of a Conference. Medford, Mass.: Fletcher School of Law and Diplomacy (February).

ROSECRANCE, R. (1971) "Some notes on problems of European security." Proceedings of the twenty-first Pugwash Conference, Sinaia, August 26-31.

SMART, I. (1972) "West European deterrence." Roundtable (April): 197-198.

SOLZHENITSYN, A. (1972) Nobel Prize Essay.

TATU, M. (1972) Le Triangle Washington-Moscou-Peking et les Deux Europes. Paris: Casterman.

VALSALICE, L. (1972) I Rapporti Cino-Americani e L'Unione Sovietica Civitas.

WYLE, F. (1972) "The United States and West European security." Survival (January-February).

––– (1970) "Is European security negotiable? " Roundtable (April).